The Martha Graham Dance Company

The Martha Graham Dance Company

House of the Pelvic Truth

Blakeley White-McGuire

methuen | drama
LONDON · NEW YORK · OXFORD · NEW DELHI · SYDNEY

METHUEN DRAMA
Bloomsbury Publishing Plc
50 Bedford Square, London, WC1B 3DP, UK
1385 Broadway, New York, NY 10018, USA
29 Earlsfort Terrace, Dublin 2, Ireland

BLOOMSBURY, METHUEN DRAMA and the Methuen Drama logo are
trademarks of Bloomsbury Publishing Plc

First published in Great Britain 2022

Cover design: Ben Anslow
Cover image: The Martha Graham Dance Company in *Night Journey* as
The Daughters of the Night. Dancers: Laurel Dalley Smith, Leslie Andrea Williams,
So Young An, Anne O'Donnell, Anne Souder, and Charlotte Landreau.
Photograph © Ken Browar and Deborah Ory.

A catalogue record for this book is available from the British Library.

A catalog record for this book is available from the Library of Congress.

ISBN: HB: 978-1-3501-4587-0
       PB: 978-1-3501-4586-3
       ePDF: 978-1-3501-4588-7
       eBook: 978-1-3501-4589-4

Typeset by Integra Software Services Pvt. Ltd.
Printed and bound in Great Britain

To find out more about our authors and books visit www.bloomsbury.com
and sign up for our newsletters.

Any great art is the condensation of a strong emotion:
a perfectly conscious thing.
—Martha Graham (1927)

This book was researched and written during the pandemic
of 2020–1 on the unceded ancestral land of the
Leni Lanape people, also known as the island of
Manhattan, New York City.

To my family in blood and spirit for believing
that everything is possible; for holding the space
for me to stand tall.

I dance my gratitude and thanksgiving to you.

To my fellow dancers of all forms and expressions.
Our sacred experiences of the body's mystery, majesty,
and power binds us together through time and generations.

And …

I would like to acknowledge Dana Mills
for her unwavering confidence in me.

This book would not have been written without
your interventions.

Thank you, Dana.

CONTENTS

FIGURES

Preface

There were few opportunities to study modern dance techniques in South Louisiana, United States of America where I was born and raised. Luckily, a presenting partnership between the regional Baton Rouge Ballet Theater and Louisiana State University's Dance Department provided me a life-changing opportunity to see the Martha Graham Ensemble perform live in my native home. The repertory consisted of three classic Graham choreographies *El Penetinte*, *Helios* from *Acts of Light*, and *Diversion of Angels*. I also took my first Graham master class that day with dancer Sandra Kaufmann. After that I became deeply curious about Martha Graham, the dancer/artist. The sophistication of and symbolism in her work inspired me to move. Soon after I was on my way to New York, to a new life. I was eighteen years old.

I consider it a gift and a privilege to have had access to the dances, technique, and personal lineage that is embodied through the Martha Graham Dance Company. During my career with the Company (2001–16, 2017) and before that with the Martha Graham Ensemble[1] (1995–6), I danced as chorus, soloist and principal dancer interpreting the roles which Graham created for herself. That body of work facilitated the development of my stage presence as well as my emotional capacity to execute the literature of Graham's repertory. I earned a wealth of knowledge about communicating in the sacred language of human movement. Graham's canon provided agency for me to feel my female dancing body as powerful and beautiful, as a subject for discovery rather than an object. Her movements came not only from herself but also from those dancers who worked with her and who gave significant time in their own lives to help her develop the technique and repertory. Thanks to this community of lineage, the Graham technique of modern dance is available for all bodies to access. Graham's canon is in the DNA of contemporary concert dance; her work has had a generational impact on many contemporary dance companies around the world including Batsheva in Israel, the Alvin Ailey American Dance Theater, Paul Taylor's American Modern Dance and Buglisi Dance Theater in New York, Cloud Gate in Taiwan, and London Contemporary Dance in the United Kingdom.

---

[1] The second company which at that time performed in New York dance seasons and international touring under Director Kazuko Hirabayashi.

Martha Graham died before I arrived as an aspirant to her "House of The Pelvic Truth." It was there that I learned to initiate movement from the deep center of the body where human life begins. Crossing the threshold of Graham's brownstone on 63rd Street and Second Avenue in New York City, I had no idea what I was stepping into but somehow it felt familiar. There, students and teachers were devoted to trying to understand Graham's philosophies of movement. I met people from around the world who had come to learn her technique of modern dance. During a transformative period in my life when I still thought of myself as a girl, I was seen and addressed as a woman. The Martha Graham Center of Contemporary Dance was the place where I learned that a particular approach to physicality can shape one's perception of life itself. I could not have known, however, how deeply her philosophies, physical technique and humanistic dances would weave into my personal life, artistic expression and career. Martha Graham wrote: "the vessel through which dance is performed is also the one through which life is lived."[2] Indeed, it is impossible to separate the two. Whenever I dance a Graham work, teach or take a Graham class, I am performing a sacred action in my life.

[2] Graham, *Blood Memory.*

Introduction

I did not choose to become a dancer, I was chosen and
with that you live all of your life.

—*Martha Graham*

FIGURE 1 *Martha Graham in* Deep Song. *Photograph by Barbara Morgan.*

Modern dancer and choreographer Martha Graham (1894–1991) devoted her life to the practical work of creating art with the dancing body. She was born in Allegheny, Pennsylvania and died in New York City, NY. Her father was a doctor of nervous disorders, a psychiatrist. Her mother held the traditional Western role for a woman, bearing four children; three girls (Martha was the eldest) and a boy who died in early childhood. In her autobiography, *Blood Memory* (Doubleday Publishing, 1991) Graham recounts her experiences of a childhood full of history, a love for animals and a closeness with her father in particular. As a girl, she moved with her family across North America from Pennsylvania in the East to Santa Barbara, California in the West. This adventure made a great impact upon what would later become her artistic aesthetics including her use of imagistic expansive space and a direct horizontal gaze in her dances.

Her first dance training began around 1916 when she enrolled at The Denishawn School of Dance and Related Arts founded by Ruth St. Denis and her husband Ted Shawn in Los Angeles, California. There she would begin her life as an artist. She eventually returned East to New York City where she found work dancing in the Greenwich Village Follies. In forming her company she laid a foundation that would make her one of the most celebrated creative minds of the twentieth century. In the early to mid-twentieth century, modern dance developed from a personal practice of discovery into a performing art genre. It formed primarily (but not exclusively) in New York City through a unique societal interplay of The Great Depression, immigration, activism in civil rights; including women's suffrage, and the development of psychology.[1] Graham saw desperate people standing on breadlines and used those images in her early dances such as *Chronicle* (1936). Many of her early dancers were the children of Jewish immigrants and refugees fleeing persecution and war. In a time when the United States was at war with Japan, and the inhuman practice of apartheid was still enforced in parts of the United States, Graham created a company that employed dancers based on content of their work not on the color of their skin. She lived as an independent woman, married for a time to choreographer Erik Hawkins, but she remained childless in a time when women still held very traditional roles in US society. Artists search for new definitions behind accepted symbols; she was an artist interrogating our human experience during the modern era.

Choreographers at that time mined the body for information; many developed physical vocabularies and aesthetics through collaborative experimentations. In its nascency, the genre manifested through individual artists such as Graham, Doris Humphrey, Charles Weidman, Katherine Dunham, Pearl Primus, Michio Ito, Lester Horton, Mary Wigman, and many others who were devoted to developing codified techniques and dances for repertory performance groups. Themes of humanism, spiritual endurance, mysticism, political unrest, and the power of masses to transgress societal

---

[1] See Graff, *Stepping Left*.

norms dominated early works. Through the dance practice of transmitting lineal knowledge in the master/apprentice model, many of the dances and practices of the period are still accessible. At this writing, thirty years after her death, Graham's voice in particular still resonates vibrantly through an artistic canon of repertory, codified dance technique and philosophies for living as a dancer in the modern world. Her dances celebrate the vitality of human emotion using movement as medium. Through its breadth and scope, Graham's canon empowers its practitioners to embrace their physical power and artistic expressions, sometimes in the face of oppressive societal norms.

A dancing body functions in discourse with personal stories, desires, and latent potential. Dancing reveals aspects of a person where words fall short. To dance is a primary human inheritance; the role of the dancer is to bring this wealth to mind. As Graham said countless times in in varying contexts throughout her life "movement never lies." She shared the genesis of this affirmation in her autobiography, *Blood Memory* (1991), a compendium of previously published writings compiled with her editor, Jacqueline Kennedy Onassis. Graham wrote that it was her father who first revealed to her an awareness of the relationship between one's inner life and outer movements. She wrote "Each of us tells our own story even without speaking. 'Movement' he told me ... 'never lies.'" Time and time again, whether in her writings or interviews, Graham attributed this primary lesson from her father as the beginning of her life as a dancer. It was a fascination that unleashed a force of nature that was her dancing body and mind.

Affirmations from Martha Graham 1926–37

Reading through personal journals from my time as a student at the Martha Graham Center in New York City, I found a list of affirmations on dancing titled, *Affirmations from Martha Graham 1926–37*. These were given to me during a pedagogy course at the Graham School in the early 1990s led by the gracious and beautiful Diane Gray (principal dancer 1963–71, and director of the School from 1983–97). Although the original source material for these affirmations were not annotated, the source from which they came to me is primary. Because they are written in my penmanship, it is possible that they are not verbatim but rather *in the spirit of*. Any scholar or student of Graham will recognize the spirit of the artist in the following paraphrased notes:

- *The gesture is the thing truly expressive of the individual, as we think, so we will act (1926).*

- *Civilization has made it impossible and undesirable for us to lead the rugged, hardy lives of our ancestors, but in the place of physical adventure, which kept them alert, alive to the very finger tips, we have a hundred-fold more mental adventures, which serve the same purpose of quickening our pulses and vitalizing our energies.*

- *Any dance, however formal and stylized in its manifestation, which does not stem from life itself will become decadent.*
- *One has to become what one is.*
- *If you can write the story of your dance, it is a literary thing but not dance (1936).*
- *There is a necessity for movement when words are not adequate.*
- *The basis of all dancing is something deep within you.*[2]

The specificity of Graham's intention in these ideas is significant because they relate to dance as an art form and the dancer as artist. She articulates with words that dance must be experienced as an expression in its own right. Dance, the action itself, is the poetry of movement. Where spoken word has been shaped into poetic expression on the page, so too has movement on the stage.

The Martha Graham Center of Contemporary Dance, her namesake dance company and school, enabled her to develop her creative potential; providing a home/space for creating, and for gathering in artistic community. She was revered as an iconic artist during her lifetime. Her enduring legacy and artistic influence continues to transcend time and space in the worlds of dance, visual art, theater, and beyond. Developmental Psychologist Howard Gardner, in his book *Creating Minds*, highlights Martha Graham as a female creative genius in the company of several men including Albert Einstein, Pablo Picasso, Igor Stravinksy, T. S. Eliot, and Mahatma Gandhi. He writes:

> Moreover, because Graham's appeal lay so significantly in her person, she may have loomed larger as a figure during her life than she will in the next century ... Because she had virtually created a new domain and had stimulated the development of a complementary field, Graham had available a capacious expanse on which to express herself, and she took full advantage of its breadth. Her originality continued unabated for many decades. In some ways her task was more difficult than Picasso's, because as a performer, and later as a leader, she had to mobilize herself and her group at historical moments to be in full readiness in a way that creators in other domains need not be. Her creative essence could not be dissociated from her physical presence.

(277, 308)

While Gardner's prediction of her presence waning after death proved accurate, the body of work itself endures. The continued resonance of Graham's canon, as presented here in further chapters, is a testament to its generative transcendent power. She was a firebrand. Her vast body of

---

[2] Quotes attributed to Martha Graham from the student journal of Blakeley White-McGuire.

work includes a roster of 181 dances as well as her espoused philosophies documented through published writings and films. The visual art and musical compositions made by her collaborators, who were also sought-after artists of their time, became inextricable by-products of her dances. She planted seeds of artistic inspiration into the imaginations of generations of dancers who, upon leaving her company, created their own, founded schools, and directed dance programs.

Artists who have danced with the Martha Graham Dance Company or studied the technique in depth hold valuable, first-hand knowledge which contribute to the field of Arts and Humanities and Choreographic Epistemology as a whole. These individuals continue to teach the internationally celebrated technique not only at The Martha Graham Center of Contemporary Dance in New York City, but also in world-renowned conservatories including Juilliard, Purchase Conservatory, RUDRA in Switzerland, Taipei Normal University, The Ailey School, Ecole de Danse de L'Opéra National de Paris, Middlesex University, Trinity/Laban, and The Greek National School of Dance. Many high schools, conservatories, and other college programs also continue the work of opening the imaginations of new generations of dance students to the Graham technique. Forward-looking and generative, Martha Graham knew and described her work as contemporary dance because she was expressing her dance of the now.

Stepping into a Life

In dance, there is no great choreographer without great dancers. This is a fundamental truth of the lineage. What are the tools of a modern dancer? Emotion, physical body, space, setting, costuming, music, and most of all, imagination. A typical day in the life of a Graham dancer begins with conscious breathing exercises in technique class and ends with either a six-hour rehearsal day or a performance. During that time, a dancer is developing strength and stamina and also opening themselves for direction from their coaches. From morning to night, the dancer is priming themself for sacred action.

The "dancer's walk" is a perfect example of the sacred action. Walking, if one is able to do so, like breathing is natural, functional, and ubiquitous in everyday life. However, in dance as in life there can be many characteristics to a walk. Graham's walk requires a shift of weight past a natural gait. Each person has their own way of shifting from place to place but the dancer's walk requires an acute awareness and intention to push past the point of departure from deep within the pelvic center. Energetically connecting with the earth through the legs while simultaneously reaching the crown of the head up toward the sky, one must lift the body up against the pull of gravity. I remember vividly practicing "the dancer's walk" from Bloomingdale's department store on the Upper East Side of Manhattan all the way down to my small studio apartment in the West Village. Practicing and trying to perfect the dancer's walk gave me purpose and a feeling of dignity during a time in my life as a young woman when I was searching for my voice, for my dance. Each step brought me toward my highest self through cultivated action in space and time. "Graham demands that you be one hundred times your best self," says Virginie Mécène, Director of Graham 2, the junior company. I agree. That is what the training is for, to become one hundred times our best selves.

At the time of my training, Graham's force of will and influence were palpable within the community. It was infectious! With the help of my teachers and by viewing live performances of the Company, I found that my imagination could bring not only Graham's ideas to life but my own as well. Through learning and practicing her technique I revealed my strong sensual body; not as an exhibition but as a personally dignified expression of self-empowerment. To me, dance philosophies, physical technique, and performance repertory are affirmations of the existential importance of passing on lineal knowledge to new generations of dancers. Through physical activation either as performer or audience, these movements re-make me each time I engage them. It is a theatrical lineage of choice, and membership is achieved only through the effort of doing.

Imagery is also vital to our work in the Graham technique and repertoire. In the following examples I describe some of the most important exercises within the technique. These create pathways in the body-mind; enabling a dancer to understand how to approach the work through activating significant physical qualities.

Fundamental Exercises of the Technique

The following list is not and is not intended to be exhaustive. It is rather a sampling of my interpretations of exercises that I engage as part of my daily dance and teaching practices. There are many published books, videos and institutional curricula that have fully documented the technique.

- *Pulses/bounces*: Feet are pressed together like a prayer; hands hold the ankles. This first conditioning exercise in Graham class has the dancer drop the crown of the head forward over the feet into a deepening stretch of the spine. Opening the inside/out from the center, the body expands and deepens simultaneously. Just as a seed nestles into the dirt and starts to grows from that place, the spine lengthens out into space on a diagonal from the pelvis, finally rising up to vertical in order to begin again.
- *Breathings*: These breathings take the body from the curved contraction into the elongated release of the spine in a simple movement that

requires complete focus. The simple act of breathing brings us to experience renewal at the beginning of every class. It reminds us that the body is a miracle. Breathing presents possibility for new thought patterns and can be a method for re-calibrating one's relationship with the familiar in our lives.

FIGURE 2 *Dancer Clive Thompson suspended in contraction. Photograph by Jack Mitchell.*

- *Contraction/release*: The breath is exhaled from the body when a dancer "takes a contraction." This expansion lengthens the spine and shapes the body through a lift against gravity. The contraction is a physical affirmation of personal will and inner direction (see Figure 2).

- *Deep stretch*: The dancer takes a contraction, exhales with legs wide in second position, turns the body inside out. The front of the body expands, deepens over the ground into a long curve. Flexing the feet and cupping the hands, the limbs stretch in opposing directions. The release of the contraction sends the spine out into the diagonal space as the weight of the body drops through the torso and legs into the floor. Finally the torso up-rights perpendicular to the floor completing the cycle to begin again.

- *Pretzel*: The essence of this exercise lives in its multidimensional form, its deepening into the center of the body. The dancer sits with one hip stacked on top of the other, one arm is bent at the elbow and wrist bracing the knee while the other is pressing down into the floor. The form creates a sculptural shape calling to mind the art of Brancusi. Graham's deepening contraction takes the dancer around their own spine and over to the floor with the arms looped in a circle to frame the top hip. The pretzel should initiate from an exhalation into the contraction, the widening hips, the orgasmic experience of the body, and a feeling of expansion. The pretzel gives the feeling of falling into your own center.

- *Pleading*: One of the most poignant and beautiful movements within the Graham technique is the pleading. Michelangelo's *Pieta* is the image most commonly shared for inspiration when teaching this exercise. The strength in vulnerability shown in the *Pieta* touches us and creates a cathartic response. Graham's pleading does the same. Deepening into the surrender, the curve and the contraction of the body is key to the actual achievement of form and feeling in this exercise. The pleading allows for a surrender of weight into the earth. It is a physical acknowledgment of gravity, a force that we reckon with in every upright moment. Heavy with gravity, the body finds points to counter balance or cantilever related to the floor. The head hangs back yet is supported by the engagement of contraction in the center of the body; an opening of the throat denotes vulnerability.

- *Falls*: Graham said that instead of falling onto the floor, her dancers bring the floor up to meet them. If we were to fall onto the floor without opposition, the dance itself would die. By engaging the idea of the floor rising to meet the body, the fall continues into the recovery. There is a dialogue with the floor/ground, which is vital and alive.

- *Wide Stride*: The dancer begins with the right leg crossed behind the left. Keeping weight in the front leg, the back leg slips out in a wide split between the thighs with arms circling down and out. The body moves to embrace the space of its environment and projects a feeling of expansiveness.

- *Tilt*: Tilting in space is oftentimes misinterpreted as a virtuosic action to show off a dancer's leg extension; however it is not. In a tilt the dancer stands firmly on one leg with the other high in the air, but they are continually falling through space and shifting weight to the next step while maintaining the torso parallel with the ground. The extension of the leg is not intended to be the focus however, the focus should be on the shift of the torso falling and recovering in space.

- *Sparkle*: The sparkle is a jump! With both arms reaching forward from the center of the heart, and both legs stretching in full active energy behind the tailbone; the sparkle is taken on alternating legs through space. It is an expression of freedom of spirit and impossible to do without a smile.

These movements and many others have become emblematic of Graham herself and symbolic in the language of her art. Her dance expresses a primary function of art that is to illuminate the archetypes, essential and unseen, behind accepted symbols.[3] Graham illuminated new interpretations of human movement as well as ancient stories with her expressions of dance and theater and through her notable collaborations with twentieth-century giants such as sculptor Isamu Noguchi, composer Aaron Copeland, photographer Barbara Morgan, and lighting designer Jean Rosenthal. The constitution of her theater resides not only in choreographies but also the ephemera related to her dances. Singular sculptures, transcendent symphonies, groundbreaking images and lighting aesthetics born out of Graham's collaborations continue to be fertile source materials which are rediscovered anew over generations. Many of her dance ideas developed in relationship to her therapeutic practice through sessions and friendship with psychoanalyst Frances Wickes.[4] The personal discoveries she made in psychoanalysis supported her intellectual engagement with archetypes and her use of symbolism in dances. Mythologist Joseph Campbell (who was married to Graham dancer and choreographer Jean Erdman) advised Graham on world mythologies which she manifested into her theatrical imagery and staging. Choreographer Agnes DeMille writes about Campbell's work with Graham in the biography *Martha, The Life and Work of Martha Graham*. DeMille quotes Joseph Campbell: "It wasn't in *Deaths and Entrances* that her psychological concepts matured, but in her Greek pieces. The collective unconscious of Jung[5] is the dynamic of the human body, the energies of the

---

[3] Attributed to C. G. Jung.
[4] See Graham, *Blood Memory*.
[5] C. G. Jung, founder of analytical psychology.

memory." … "Jung opens the structure of the psyche to race[6] memory, the common treasurer which we all inherit. For Jung [and for Campbell] this is the basis of art; it is our common magic."[7]

Modern dance is a cultural dance practice in that it reflects aspects of its incubator society, in this case ideas of Western culture in the USA. In recognizing the ways in which this linkage manifests, we as practitioners/ audience gain insight into the potency of the work over time. Graham's daring transgressions in creating a company and dances which feature the expressive, powerful, and sensual dancing body during a time of hegemony, severe patriarchy, and legal racism in the USA are significant in framing her canon. An artist's native culture is inextricably linked to their work. Along with many other artists working during the early to mid-twentieth century, she was deeply influenced by the rituals and visual languages of Indigenous/ Native/First Nation people's cultural practices which she encountered. She acknowledged Indigenous culture as being inextricable from any "new" form of "American dance." The practice by "Americans"[8] of making work that was inspired by or in appropriation of Indigenous cultural forms is problematic for many reasons. It is also inseparable from the genre of early modern dance itself. In fact, it is nearly impossible to parcel out Graham's work or any other art work from the whole of world art because of our very human nature. Global human immigration/emigration whether by enslavement, force or personal choice blends cultures and ideas through the cycle of life and human action. Writer and Civil Rights Activist James Baldwin presents an eloquent example of art manifesting in different places and societies in his essay *Princes and Powers*. Here, Baldwin describes and paraphrases ideas on art and culture coming from Africa by the Senegalese poet, Leopold Senghor.

Baldwin writes:

He [Senghor] told us that the difference between the function of the arts in Europe and their function in Africa play in the fact that, in Africa, the function of the arts is more present and pervasive, "is infinitely less special, is done by all for all." Thus, art for our sake it's not a concept which makes any sense in Africa. The division between art and life out of which such a concept comes does not exist there. Art itself is taken to be perishable to be made again each time it disappears or is destroyed. What is clung to is the spirit which makes art possible. And the African idea of the spirit is very different from the European idea. European art attempts to imitate nature. African art is concerned with reaching beyond and beneath nature, to connect, and itself become part of *la force vitale*.[9]

---

[6] Referring to the one human race.

[7] Agnes DeMille, *Martha: The Life and Work of Martha Graham*.

[8] A term used to describe citizens of The United States of America.

[9] James Baldwin, *Price of the Ticket: Collected Nonfiction, 1948–1985* (Manhattan, NY: St. Martin's Press, 1985).

Many of the philosophies that Graham espouses in her canon hold these same core tenets. Where did she encounter them? Most likely not in her Puritan upbringing. She encountered and incorporated different aesthetics through her collaborative relationships, blended those world cultural ideas which she encountered or studied, then synthesized and developed them through her own female dancing body.

Today the modern dance community stands in the wake of the inevitable deaths of the most celebrated individualist modern concert dance innovators of the twentieth century, generally known as the pioneers of modern dance (Graham, Alvin Ailey, Merce Cunningham, Katherine Dunham, José Limón, Paul Taylor, and Pina Bausch/Tanztheater). The single-authored companies that were the genesis of the art form have either transformed and grown more encompassing of dance in general or become more exclusive and rarified. Some company managements have taken up the gauntlet of American modern dance while others have kept the focus primarily on the work of the original author/choreographer. Whatever the approach, the concert dance community is being inevitably forced to assess what remains from this most fertile period of creativity in modern dance history and how to invest in the future with its great wealth of experiential knowledge.

Thirty years after the artist's death, it is fitting and timely to examine the state of the Martha Graham Dance Company and its ongoing artistic lineage. My intention in this book is to illuminate and provide a platform for both sharing and inquiry into transformative aspects of the physical artistic practices which are accessible through the life of the Graham canon. The reader will find oral histories of company dancers who worked with Graham toward the end of her life as well as from dancers who are presently stepping into the technique and repertory. There are interviews, poems, journal entries, quotes, citations and re-publications to be discovered herein. Through its reading, we learn about artists who not only refuse to let Graham's legacy be lost, but are actively cultivating its continued development in the world of art, theater, and dance.

Dancing demonstrates respect for our bodies as the vessels which carry us through life. The call to dance and to create a world of dance for others is a demand from the inside out. We heal ourselves through our movements just as we destroy ourselves through them. In her cultivated forms of deconstructed human emotion through dance, Martha Graham made a pathway to healing and evolution. The dancers, audiences, educators, presenters, scholars, and patrons who maintain, teach, and develop her artistic practices contemporarily will determine what remains and what will fall away over time. We in the Graham lineage have not let go; in fact we have fought to keep it alive in our bodies and theaters. The work itself need only be presented in its purest form by those who have lived inside of it, who want to live inside of it, and are willing to take action.

I have studied and worked inside of the Graham canon for over twenty-six years. First as a student member the Graham Ensemble[10] under Kazuko Hirabayashi and Kenneth Topping, and then with the Martha Graham Dance Company under the direction of Terese Capucilli, Christine Dakin, and Janet Eilber. My current role as teacher and stager of Graham repertory empowers me to continue this work with dancers around the world. I recall a conversation with American choreographer Kate Weare after a company performance at the Guggenheim Museum in New York City. Weare commented that she experienced Graham's work as "will-based." She was absolutely correct because a dancer's physical investment in its form is huge by necessity; the road to developing a deeply cultivated practice is long and progress can be oftentimes slow. Lineage supports the individual and the group. It affirms the resonance of an individual voice within the work by practiced recognition; person to person, dancer to dancer, teacher to student. Graham's subject materials are deep entanglements of meaning, mythology, passion, tragedy and endurance that both performer and audience must be willing to engage and celebrate.

The development of dance depends on the will and affection of people. The only way for dance to continue is for dancers to continue. We must have spaces for training, venues in which to perform and curious audience members who are willing to embark on an unknown journey. In considering physical practice in lineage, I find support from the writer/ecologist/agrarian Wendell Berry in his essay *It All Turns on Affection*.[11] Berry eloquently expresses the urgent necessity of sharing generationally accrued knowledge. Speaking of the "cultural cycle," he brings our attention to those natural forces of decay and loss. He asks the reader to consider what is valuable and worth maintaining. In the face of natural cycles of decay and re-birth, in the constancy and inevitability of change, there are many ideas and practices worth maintaining through affection. Here, where Berry argues for agriculture, I argue the same for dance.

He writes:

In 1936, moreover, only a handful of people [in the United States] were thinking about sustainability. Now, reasonably, many of us are thinking about it. The problem of sustainability is simple enough to state. It requires that the fertility cycle of birth, growth, maturity, death, and decay — [...] "The Wheel of Life" — should turn continuously in place, so that the law of return is kept and nothing is wasted. For this to happen in the stewardship of humans, there must be a cultural cycle, in harmony with the fertility cycle, also continuously turning in place. The cultural cycle is an unending conversation between old people and young people, assuring the survival of local memory, which has, as long as it remains

---

[10] The junior performing troupe created by Yuriko Kikuchi, now known as Graham 2. It is currently directed by Virginie Mécène.

[11] 2012 National Endowment for the Arts, Jefferson Lecture.

local, the greatest practical urgency and value. This is what is meant, and is all that is meant, by "sustainability." The fertility cycle turns by the law of nature. The cultural cycle turns on affection.

In dance practice the "affection" that Berry speaks of is nurtured in the studio through class from dancer to dancer, teacher to student. Because its language is physical rather than literary it will thrive only through personal relationships and by the will, interest and affection of people. Work is a word oftentimes used by dancers when speaking about their art practice. I bring attention to this as a means of understanding a dancer's perspective. For these artists dance does not particularly need to be fun or entertaining or distracting. In fact, for Graham artists the opposite rings true. The rigorous demands of dance bring us into the raw emotion of our present realities. The physicality of our bodies in space/environment are related to time and breath with certain movements reaching out beyond our recall[12] and into our blood memory. The physical practice of connecting to our past, present, and future in each moment is the dance. Graham's practice of using the impulse of the *and count*[13] (beginning a movement before the musical beat) is a poetic reminder of the ongoing nature of our work.

"In my beginning is my end."[14] My practice as a movement artist is to do, to make, and to share. In this book, I hope to empower the reader to experience the compassion and community that dance can generate. I hope to affirm the choices, creativity, and productivity of generations of people who walked into Martha Graham's "House of The Pelvic Truth" to learn, to strengthen, and to carve out their own lives as artists in the face of all obstacles. The crucible of the canon and all of the personal trials which it presents to the artist transforms the person who chooses or is chosen. The journey is not about living in the past but rather having a platform from which to jump into one's future in community with others. Through its lineage, I have discovered beautiful aspects of my own life's work in dance. My gratitude flows over for Martha Graham and the dancers who made this world and who refused to let it burn out. The time when a dancer comes through the Company affects their experience of the canon. Each generation changes the work because of its very contemporary nature. Its philosophical foundation, however, is broad enough to support change; changes in body types, attitudes, and cultures. As it is oftentimes said in the studio, the only constant is change. And …

---

[12] Phrase inspired by Ranier Maria Rilke.

[13] The "and" is related to dynamic musical phrasing in Graham's technique, the dancer is never in the middle of a musical note or rhythmic beat, the dancer is the note; is the beat. This dynamic relationship is created by initiating a movement before the count of "1." Its effect is two-fold in that: 1) the music appears to come from the movement; and 2) the consciousness of transition and the liminality of space between the notes is always present in the dancing body-mind.

[14] T. S. Elliot, *Four Quartets: East Coker.*

1

Creating from the Inside Out: A Brief Introduction to the Martha Graham Dance Company

No artist is ever ahead of his time, he is the time. It is the rest of the world that has to do the catching up.

—*Martha Graham*

FIGURE 3 Deo *by Bobbi Jene Smith and Maxine Doyle. Dancers: Xin Ying, Leslie Andrea Williams, Anne O'Donnell, Anne Souder, Marzia Memoli, Laurel Dalley Smith, and So Young An. Photograph by Christopher Jones.*

As a girl, Martha Graham attended a performance given by the legendary dancer Ruth St. Denis. She would later say, "Ms. Ruth opened the door, I walked into a life."[1] At the Denishawn School she had studied quixotic theatricality, costuming, and thematic dances of imagined world cultures which catered to its Euro-American audiences. Although she was his student, Ted Shawn chose Martha to be his dance partner which eventually led to her star turn in the Greenwich Village Follies. There, she performed for New York City's Vaudeville audiences and began a new stage in her life. The artistic community of New York would have a significant influenced on her artistic expression and lead her into a new realm of dance.

Under the guidance of composer Louis Horst (also from Denishawn), she would find a new direction by moving away from dancing as entertainment and toward its potential as transformative art. Horst became a tremendous influence as both her musical director and friend. He pushed her hard to find new forms through her own body and introduced her to avant-garde artists and vital composers of the day. With Horst she encountered new influences from the modern art period that revealed radical possibilities and helped her to break away from Denishawn-ian concepts of dance.

In founding the Martha Graham Dance Company, Graham formed both physical and metaphysical spaces for her artistic development. Her vision of dance revealed it as not only ritual and expression but also as theater. She presented dance as a dominant form in theatrical presentations instead of as a supporting one. The company gave its first performance in 1926 with Graham and three of her students from the Eastman School of Music, Thelma Biracree, Betty Macdonald and Evelyn Sabin, dancing a program of solos and trios. This foundational relationship between dance teacher and student continues to be vital to the continuity of the Company.

Like many artists in the mid-twentieth century, Graham sought to create an original American art form coming from the ferment of place. Cultural identity and oppression were early themes in her dances such as *Heretic* (1929), *Immigrant* (1928), and *Imperial Gesture* (1935). Although she was a product of her birthplace (Pennsylvania) and childhood home (California), her vision reached beyond borders of nationality. Her dances still move us into a frontier of discovery that reveals our common and complex emotional human nature. In this excerpt from a program titled "Martha Graham and Dance Group Program,"[2] she articulated her early perspective:

It [the creation of an American dance form] requires that the choreographer sensitizes himself to his country, that he know its history, its political and geographical life, and that he direct and correlate his experiences into significant compositions of movement.

---

[1] "Martha Graham: The Dancer Revealed," *American Masters*, 1994, season 1, episode 2.
[2] Martha Graham Center of Contemporary Dance Archives.

No great dance can leave a people unmoved. Sometimes the reaction will take the form of a cold antagonism to the truth of what they are seeing –sometimes a full-hearted response. What is necessary is that the dance be as strong as the life that is known in the country. That it be influenced by the prevailing expression of its people as well as by the geography of the land itself.

She made dances with huge themes in a repertory that blended ideas from world cultural practices; Graham did not claim originality. Her artistic manifestations reflected the creative environment in New York City at the time as well as a colonizing practice that was foundational to her native United States culture. She placed theater from Europe, symbolism from Asia, and ritual from North America, one on top of another. She used imagery, styles of dress, and symbolic forms found outside of the familial culture of her childhood. Whether or not she appropriated vocabulary or symbolic language is a significant question. She acknowledged and cited her sources of inspiration and integrated her embodiment of ideas through rigorous study, practice, and development. Graham said "there is nothing new, there is nothing to be discovered, the dance need only be revealed."[3] This acknowledgment of dance as revelation rather than product prompts me to consider her self-awareness of artist as vessel rather than originator. Her revolution came in her presentation, her craft of storytelling and her leadership. Graham placed her dance as the central mode for expression in her theatrical productions rather than as ancillary or responsive one. Her repertoire exposes a devotion to dance and the human body as a vessel for the sacred rituals of human life.

Her Dances

Many artists in the 1930s made work through the lens of citizen and humanist. In *Panorama* (1935), her choreography for the female students at Bennington College, Graham structured her activist ideas into three sections. Early program notes accessed through the Martha Graham Resources archives state her thematic intentions: *Theme of Dedication*, *Imperial Theme*, and *Popular Theme*. The choreographic structure of the dance presents large groups of people moving in athletic rhythmic formations. Its actions call to mind the activism that is necessary to bring about any significant change in minds and lives of people. She writes "this theme is of the people and their awakening social consciousness in the contemporary scene."[4] The pedestrian movements of *Panorama* are accessible to untrained movers and named for basic forms of physicality such as unison lunge

---

[3] Graham, *Blood Memory.*
[4] Program notes for *Panorama.*

switches, kneeling, walks, prances, and arm beats. Its reconstruction in the early 1990s led by the luminary dancer Yuriko, and its subsequent re-staging within the Graham community of dancers has led to its now yearly performance in the *All-City Panorama*. In this special New York City event, high school students from the five boroughs audition and are then invited to learn and perform *Panorama* in the Martha Graham Dance Company's New York performance season. New generations are embodying not only the work of art, but they are also learning about the dance his(her)story of artists in their city. The life of this work demonstrates *how* transference of accumulated knowledge circulates back into its community of origin with renewed vitality and resonance.

Looking at transference through the metaphoric lens of writing, dance scholar and political philosopher Dana Mills describes this phenomenon in her book *Dance and Politics: Moving Beyond Boundaries*. She introduces the sic-sensuous act "of writing one's body upon another body, and bodies writing upon their space" (16). Mills states:

> Dancer's bodies are also the pens with which they write on others bodies. Reading dance as a language and a way of knowing means that the body is both the instrument of writing and the surface upon which it writes [...] I argue that the strong reading of political dance is intimately intertwined with the understanding of dance as an embodied language, a method of inscription independent of words [...] sic-sensuous [is] a concept which I utilise in order to focus upon acts of writing performed by manifold bodies who have written upon the argument; the argument in turn turns the spotlight on moments of shared sensation.
>
> (15)

Mills' concept of sic-sensuous addresses both individual and communal cultural practices by examining how a dance work moves over time through one body to penetrate the body and psyche of another.

Scholar and former Graham dancer Ellen Graff describes in her book, *Stepping Left*, the conditions of the historical period when dance artists such as Graham were making dances with revolution in mind. Graff writes:

> What established their credentials as revolutionary artists was the content of the dances, the political and social commentary that emanated from the percussive thrust of a heel or a head's abrupt turn. Radical dancers may have openly embraced bourgeois technique, but they did not dance about "the life of a bee." They danced about the lives and concerns of working people.
>
> "The Worker" however was increasingly absent from the stage. In the most artistically successful efforts by revolutionary dancers, the worker was an imagined inhabitant of a trained body rather than a participant in

the experience ... What established their art as revolutionary was content; in essence, their dances were narratives about crises affecting the worker. (75)

Frontier (1935) is a joyous dance of a young girl indulging her dreams and exploring her desires to answer the call to adventure. It embodies an attitude *I will, I can, yes*. Movements in this minimalist work develop as simple variations on a theme. Graham mined the universal emotional experiences of joy, excitement, and desire in her work. While there is nothing ordinary about the dances of Martha Graham, many of her early themes did speak to the everyday inner life of people. The frontier, whether in space or imagination, is another theme in her dances. The landscape and imagined possibilities are synthesized through her outbursts of high kicks, jumps, small skitters and pumping heel lifts. In the dance, the beauty of the landscape brings the girl to her knees.

The gestures are intensified by the simplicity of Isamu Noguchi's set designs and the resolute snare drum beat of Louis Horst's musical composition. Sculptor Isamu Noguchi (1904–88) built many of the environments for Graham's dances including *Frontier* and *Appalachian Spring* (1944). Noguchi's stage setting for *Frontier* is a simple free-standing link of log fence and a cotton rope. The rope shapes the space stretching out in a V from the upstage center of the floor seemingly into infinity. Noguchi said "I used a rope, nothing else, it is not the rope that is the sculpture, but it is the space which it creates that is the sculpture. It is an illusion of space" ("Tribute to Martha Graham").

Space is another reoccurring thematic idea for Graham. In her autobiography she described significant influences on her (some relating to space) including the particularly molding experience of moving across North America by train from Pennsylvania to California. It was a life-altering journey out of the settled East of North America into the West. She describes feeling the wildness of the landscape in her imagination and in her body.

The train was taking us from our past, through the vehicle of the present, to our future. Tracks in front of me, how they gleamed whether we went straight ahead or through a newly carved-out mountain. It was these tracks that hugged the land, and became a living part of my memory. Parallel lines whose meaning was inexhaustible, whose purpose was infinite. This was for me the beginning of my ballet Frontier.[5]

The individual self in relationship to the landscape is at the heart of *Frontier*; its ethos is simply human. The girl in *Frontier* is a settler. Graham amplifies her emotional experience, her boldness, and her quickening of spirit.

---

[5] Graham, *Blood Memory*.

Her gestures are set against a backdrop of intentional, systematic erasure of Indigenous people's histories by settlers. The genesis of the United States of America as a nation of settlers seeking to claim land and dominate Indigenous cultures is inherent in much of US-American art; is an existential reality of the art itself. This history is unseen yet expressed in the feeling and sound of discord that wafts in and out of *Frontier*. The dancer is answering the call to explore the unknown and all that that adventure conjures. Much like Thoreau, Graham relates the untamed wildness of North America with an inner awakening. Author Dana Mills concurs, "Just as the Founding Fathers sought to establish both a new political system and landscape, so artists sought to build a cultural life appropriate for such a new republic" (56). " Two stages need to be distinguished: the perception of the landscape by the artist and the subsequent perception of the [art] by the view" (63).

In *Appalachian Spring*, Graham uses symbolism in costuming from the pioneering period as well as Noguchi's skeleton-like structure of a town to indicate time, form, and temporality. This dance tells the story of towns folk celebrating the marriage of a young couple. Set outdoors, we encounter several characters whose archetypes are still alive and well in contemporary life: The Bride, The Husbandman, The Pioneering Woman, The Preacher and his followers. *Appalachian Spring* mines under the surface of a dominant Euro-American culture to uncover layers of life histories rumbling beneath the mask of "civilization." As an immigrant to North American many times removed, Graham herself was very aware of the histories violence and displacement actualized by the misguided and violent idea of Manifest Destiny. In her book *The People Have Never Stopped Dancing*,[6] author Jacquline Shea Murray reveals this sensitivity to the absence of the whole story of America. I recommend Murray's book, specifically the essay "We can never escape the sense of her having been here: Evoking Indians in Appalachian Spring." Murray cites one of the many letters from Graham to composer Aaron Copeland discussing the libretto which Graham wrote for *Appalachian Spring*: "... And yet she is always with us in the names of our cities, rivers, states ... This Indian Girl's absent presence – initially envisioned as emerging from the shadows, at times invisible to the woman [the Bride], but then left out of the final version of the ballet – continues to haunt *Appalachian Spring*" (157). This strong political reading of *Appalachian Spring* resonates with me as a performer who has lived in the dance because within the commonly accepted idealized story of colonized America there are so many layers for the artist to reveal. Graham presented this complex world to us in her seemingly simplistic *Appalachian Spring*.

Another dance, *Lamentation* (1930), reveals Graham's deconstruction of the innermost depths of grief as a woman stares into the void of an empty womb. Pressing out against her costuming, an ever-contracting tube

---

[6] Shea Murray, *The People Have Never Stopped Dancing: Native American Modern Dance Histories.*

of material, Graham said it was as if she was "stretching inside her own skin." The woman's veiled focus and deep contracting body bring to mind barrenness or miscarriage. Graham was excavating emotions which were kept out of public conversation in the 1930s. Using the fabric as a theatrical device, she literally and metaphorically stretches beyond her known form.[7]

Graham's dance theater is a theatrical vehicle for self-empowerment where she casts herself in a dramatic array of roles across a wide spectrum of human experiences. This desire and impetus toward embodying the space of other was fueled by her curiosity and emboldened her tenacity. She lived over the course of nearly one hundred generative years, was auto-didactic, a voracious reader, and student of literature and world art. She ardently engaged with Carl Jung's ideas on the role of human sexuality which espoused that "the libido was not just sexual energy, but instead generalized psychic energy [which could] motivate the individual in a number of important ways, including spiritually, intellectually, and creatively."[8] Graham absolutely galvanized those energies of libido and harnessed the energy into her own outrageous creativity in *Phaedra* (1962) where the theatrical settings by Isamu Noguchi enthusiastically evoke the male phallus and female vulva.

FIGURE 4 Phaedra. *Dancers: Katherine Crockett as Phaedra and XiaoChuan Xie as Aphrodite. Photograph by Paul B. Goode.*

---

[7] Graham, *Blood Memory.*
[8] C. G. Jung *The phenomenology of the spirit in fairy tales.*

Throughout her long life, Martha Graham developed her work in various identifiable periods. These include stark modernist humanism, cultural rituals, American-ist themes and her Greek Cycle exploring archetypes in mythology, the human unconscious, and heroic women in world literature. She commissioned musical scores from Aaron Copeland, Carlos Surinach, Gian Carlo Menotti, William Schuman, and Paul Hindemith among others. Later in life she accepted commissions to choreograph to pre-existing scores such as in *Acts of Light* by Danish composer Carl Nielsen (the three musical selections were originally titled *Helios Overture*, *At the Bier of a Young Artist*, and *Pan and Syrinx*). Graham also choreographed using music to which she had significant relationships such as Igor Stravinsky's the *Rite of Spring*[9] and Scott Joplin's *Maple Leaf Rag*.

She used settings and fabrics that were available and affordable to her. In *Lamentation* wool jersey was the perfect technology for showing the tension of grief and how it works upon a body from the inside out. Her use of the spaces between forms in Isamu Noguchi's settings for both *Frontier* and *Errand Into The Maze* (1947) is masterful. In these dances she shapes the audience perspective using her small body set against the backdrop of infinite spaces. Noguchi speaks of Graham's relationship to his settings:

> *I would say that with regard to my sets ... she so absorbed them completely that I could not claim they were mine, for they were hers. They were parts of her anatomy, so to speak, and she could use them in ways that I could not even imagine ... my interest was to see how sculpture might be in the hypothetical space of theater as a living part of human relationships. You see that was my particular interest and has always remained so.*[10]

In her lifetime, Graham saw and lived through tremendous upheaval and reordering of societies around the world. Accordingly, she made bold choices in her subject matter that reflected her life and times. At a time when she refused a personal invitation from Adolf Hitler for her company to perform at the 1936 Olympic Opening Ceremony in Berlin, she embodied the tragedy and anguish of war in her all-female *tour de force*, *Chronicle* (1936). Before the height of the United States' Civil Rights Movement Graham and her racially integrated company refused to perform for segregated audiences. She writes about this event in her memoir, *Blood Memory*:[11]

---

[9] Martha Graham was The Chosen One in Leonide Massine's US Premier of *Rite of Spring* in 1930.

[10] Isamu Noguchi, "Tribute to Martha Graham."

[11] It is not my intention to frame Martha Graham as an activist in any way. Rather this excerpt is intended to demonstrate that she was engaged in using her influence as an ally. Undoubtedly her focus was on herself and her work. However, through her life's work she did provide a space for individuals to cultivate their art, strength, tenacity, and beauty in a culture of white supremacy, erasure, and misogyny.

FIGURE 5 *Stage settings by Isamu Noguchi for* Errand into the Maze. *Photograph courtesy of Martha Graham Resources.*

... my company and I toured the South prior to the Civil Rights Movement, and performed at Spelman College. I told the young women of the all-black college that I would see them at the evening performance. They said, "Oh no, we can't go to the theater. It is for whites only." I went directly to the impresario. It was his first sellout and I said, "I understand you have sold out for the night." "Yes," he replied, "for the first time." I said, "That is simply wonderful. I want twenty seats for tonight's performance." He asked why and I said, "For the students at Spelman College. Otherwise there will be no performance. " Impossible," he cried. And with that I told my dancers and crew to pack up. There would be no show that night. The impresario panicked and changed his mind. Within a few minutes I had twenty seats for the women of Spelman College.

(37)

These anecdotes do not frame Graham, a white woman as a social activist; rather they situate her and her actions within the society that she was working at the time. Her focus was on her work, not on liberating others; however she was obviously aware of social injustices and inequities and did make actions that affirmed her humanism beyond her art production.

In 1967, at the age of seventy-six, Martha Graham retired from the stage. She continued working with her company to create thirty-two additional dances while battling with personal demons of alcohol and depression. She completed her final choreography at the age of ninety-six. This statement from the Martha Graham Center encapsulates her scope of influence in a simple and concise way, "Martha Graham and her company have expanded contemporary dance's vocabulary of movement and forever altered the scope of the art form by rooting works in contemporary social, political, psychological, and sexual contexts, deepening their impact and resonance."[12]

Early Collaborators

Dance is not a solitary art form. Martha Graham created 181 ballets in her lifetime but she did not accomplish this achievement alone. As has been done throughout humanity, dance in Graham's canon was made and re-made in community. The most potent expression of her work has always come from within the community of the Martha Graham Dance Company. The company is a force of artistic innovation and a repository for historical works to be re-staged and reimagined. Its legacy of engagement with human emotion is its most vital aspect.

Ten years is about the span of the career for leading dancers in the Company. Longer for some and more brief for others. Many dancers, when they took leave, became teachers and some founded dance companies of their own. The roots of the concert dance world today can be traced back to those early dancers from the 1950s, 1960s, and 1970s who struck out in all directions to disseminate their form of dance internationally. Graham's artistic diaspora spans the globe from Israel to England to Taiwan thanks to those dancers and her sound technique for developing a healthy dancing body.

The dancers in her early company laid the foundation for the artistic house of the pelvic truth. Concert dance is theater for the people; not as dictated by a king or queen, it is rather dance coming out of people who imagine their place in the world and are speaking to that world. Graham created a path of empowerment which we dancers still walk today.

The following excerpts from *Dance Magazine, Special Issue: Martha Graham* (July 1991) are interviews with Graham dancers from the 1940s to the 1990s, most of whom are now deceased. I have chosen this array of brief insights from these particular voices because each of these dancers/choreographers/teachers effected the technique, repertory, and the world of concert dance in meaningful and lasting ways.

Eric Hawkins (1909–94) was Martha Graham's husband (1948–54) and a choreographer in his own right. Here he speaks about his time with Graham:

---

[12] Martha Graham Dance Center promotional materials.

FIGURE 6 Steps in the Street. *Lead dancer: Leslie Andrea Williams with the Martha Graham Dance Company. Photograph by Christopher Jones.*

I came to Balanchine because of Serenade; I came to Martha because of *Primitive Mysteries* (1931), which I saw. It was an unusual dance because of its poetic emphasis; she never did a poetic dance quite like that later on. It was seeing her works that led me to Bennington. I guess it was because of the freedom and the boldness of her dances, which people didn't understand – they saw it as being iconoclastic, but I saw it as being a bold new statement, which reinforced my determination to be bold, and very soon to strike out on new ground myself. It was Martha's courage as an artist and as a human being that reinforced my own feelings. I think that later on she got kind of fed up with trying to be so courageous – you can get tired of that. The first dance I did with Martha was *American Document* (1938); the *Song of Solomon* duet that she and I did changed the way she worked, because my being a man let Martha be a woman, [*sic*], and in that role her dancing changed. It opened up a whole new world for me, and it was a turning point in American dance. She came into her own as a woman and she had someone like myself to take the other side of passion … She had tremendous courage that showed itself in many different ways.
(42)

Merce Cunningham and Paul Taylor were early male dancers in the Martha Graham Dance Company; Cunningham in the 1930s and 1940s and Taylor in the 1950s. Each man developed iconic roles within the repertoire. Cunningham was the original Preacher in *Appalachian Spring* and Paul Taylor danced Tiresias in the The Criterion Collection's 1959 filmic version of *Night Journey* among other works. Upon leaving Graham, both men went on to found their own namesake companies. Merce Cunningham rebelled against Graham completely, instituting chance dance as a method of choreographing, while Paul Taylor embraced his lyricism and musicality after initially breaking out as a postmodernist minimalist in the 1960s. They shared their endearing memories of their one-time director in the same article from *Dance Magazine*:

Merce Cunningham (1919–2009), Choreographer:

Martha Graham was an extraordinary dancer. She was making a form of theater that was original and distinctly American. Thinking back on my first years in New York, I realize now, as I did then, how fortunate it was for me to be on the same stage with her. She was small in stature but large in presence. Dancing with her, I had no impression of the difference between our heights. Those few years working with her and being in her company provided an experience of the dance that was not available elsewhere then. I have always been grateful for it.

(42)

Paul Taylor (1930–2018), Choreographer:

I thought I was Martha Graham – a lot of people do. A lot of people admire her so much that when they make dances they look Graham-esque ... From the word "go" I was aware that I didn't want to be another Martha Graham ... The tradition that's passed from one generation to another in modern dance – a real family – has helped me very much ... I'm her rightful son. She didn't leave me the studio, as she should have, but we are a family and I am her son.

(45)

Mary Hinkson (1925–2014) was a dancer, director, and educator in the Graham Company who was acclaimed for her beauty and aesthetic lines; she brought a noted elegance to her roles. Ms. Hinkson spoke about her time with Graham:

When I first studied with Martha it was a June course; the studio was so hot, and we were absolutely reeking of perspiration. She said, "Stop sweating! It's pure indulgence." She supposedly didn't like to teach, but her classes were so meaningful; it just seemed as though she was always creating while teaching. There was no such thing as being low-keyed; you could never feel low-keyed in Martha's presence ... Technically she created a whole body language, instead of imitating or reducing or enlarging pantomimic movement. Instead of reenacting what people do, she created a movement idiom that had within it inherent points of departure for meaning. When I was with her, I always had the impression that I was in the presence of a seer—someone whose knowledge was greater than that of the average human being.

(44)

Yuriko Kikuchi (1920–) is a dancer, choreographer, historical researcher/re-constructor, author, and educator who danced in the Company during Graham's most prodigious periods as a choreographer:

She was one of the most changeable persons; she flowed with the time, she never resisted change. She smelled the future. She and Balanchine always were one step ahead of their time. The great ones are animals—creative animals—and they sense the time they live in. When she saw new bodies coming into the studio, she changed the technique. But the technique is so fundamental; it comes from the basic behavior of the human body. Inside the body is a mechanism that is constantly doing contraction and release—the heart, the lungs, the digestive system. And giving birth is contraction and release.

(43)

Bertram Ross (1920–2003) was a Graham dancer, director, and educator. He was Martha Graham's partner in many dances including *Night Journey*:

In every new piece I did, she would say, "I want you to move in a way you've never moved before." In *Seraphic Dialogue* (1955), the way I used my hands came out of that. She did not like demonstrating for a man because she did not have a man's body—she would give it to me verbally.

(44)

Tim Wengerd (1937–82), Dancer, Choreographer:
   A beloved interpreter of Graham's male-identified roles known for his dramatic intensity and beauty. In his essay for this same issue of *Dance Magazine*, Wengerd wrote about his first encounter with the Martha Graham Dance Company in San Francisco in 1966:

By 1966, Martha Graham has assembled a company remarkable not only for its level of accomplishment, but also for its diversity of both physicality and emotional make-up ... As the performance of *Clytemnestra* revealed itself, the images of Martha's Men were branded in my skull, and I dreamed of becoming one of them. They were allowed to be all me—the sensuous and poetic, as well as macho, cruel, unfeeling creatures. The works made over a period of fifty years by this Goddess of Duplicity in her quest for truth about the human condition. On Martha's stage, being a male dancer seemed the most honorable and elevated calling, one worthy of a deep dedication and commitment. And it did not matter to me which characters I would be: Any of them would do.

(48–9)

Early on in my nine years with her, it became clear to me that dancing for Martha was not simply a matter of doing the right steps at the appropriate moment, nor even of assuming the character being danced: This was to be major psychotherapy and also a deep sharing of life itself.

(49)

John Butler (1918–93), Dancer, Choreographer, talks about his enchantment with Graham as an artist in his interview with Marian Horosko that:[13]

Something I could never understand, however, concerned her use of music. While I am so influenced by and responsive to music, I find it still a mystery that she was not. She would rehearse pieces of a dance in a studio and then commission a composer to prepare the accompaniment to that section. As always, she wrote the libretto for the entire dance, and Samuel Barber or Gian Carlo Menotti or whoever appeared to be utterly baffled when it was put together and it all seemed to work. Even if Martha denied to do her slowest passages to their liveliest sections, the contrast matched the libretto as an underlining or underscoring of her intent ... What I learned from her, and from all this, was pure theater. I responded more to her sense of drama than to her movements (I never had great technique). She was so articulate and had a capacity for such diverse imagery that I learned from her how to get the dramatic moment with honesty, brevity, and clarity – just as she did. When she directed you, she reached into your being to get the strength she know you had. You always grew with her. That's the reason I kept coming back to perform in the Company between my own seasons and commissions ...

Working with her was a double act of faith. She trusted you with her theater and you gave it back to her. You had to reach her plateau; she demanded nothing less. In turn, you found yourself making the same demands of others when you were entrusted to direct them. The legacy is handed down in this way. It is a sacred trust that works on sacred ground.

(47)

---

[13] "Martha's Prince: An Interview with Marian Horosko," *Dance Magazine, Special Issue: Martha Graham*, July 1991.

2

The Artist: Interrogating Martha Graham's Words and Works

A dance is one instant of life—a vibratory piece of energy.
—*Martha Graham (in 1985)*[1]

When entering into the metaphysical space of Graham's theater and dance, one inevitable philosophy one will encounter is this, "There is no competition except with the self you know you can become ... There is only one of you in all time, and if you do not share it with the world, it will be lost. The world will not have it."[2] These fundamental ideas in discovering oneself as a Graham artist have become part of the literature of modern dance. Time, willingness, curiosity, and reverence for the body in space are the demands of a dancer's life. Graham revealed the dance and dancer as sacred expressions that move us toward personal discoveries though embodiment. I never met Martha Graham. What I know is her art, those constitutional aspects that comprise her body of work, what they signify to me, and how to share and develop them. Her singular technique continues to build my strong dancing body-voice. I dance within her canon as myself, as Blakeley White-McGuire, not pretending to be Martha Graham or wanting to be like Martha Graham. I speak a language that engages my body-mind-imagination through ideas that her body physically rendered.

Poetic philosophies for living as an artist are foundational to the contemporary life of the Martha Graham Dance Company. In this chapter I share a variety of viewpoints from practitioners who are steeped in the life of dance and the dancing body, artists' voices that articulate the continuing importance of both the Graham Company and School. Included here are interviews with Terese Capucilli and Christine Dakin (co-Artistic Directors of the MGDC from 2002 to 2005), both renowned as master interpreters

---

[1] *Good Morning America* interview with Martha Graham.
[2] Graham, *Blood Memory*.

of Graham's principal roles and muses for Graham in her final completed works. Principal dancers Elizabeth Auclair, Katherine Crockett, and Miki Orihara, who also performed major female roles of the repertoire as the first generation of the Company after Graham's death, are also included. These dancers offer personal insight into lineage, imagery, and artistic process. A current member of the Company, Leslie Andrea Williams, who performs leading roles in the repertoire, also speaks in this chapter. Williams is a former student of Capucilli at The Juilliard School in New York and continues to cultivate the vibrancy of lineage.

In analyzing dances and technical exercises from the canon we can find a bridge between philosophy and practice which create rituals for both teaching and learning within the lineage. The following dances will be addressed and are fine examples from Graham's diverse repertory: *Lamentation, Errand into the Maze, Cave of the Heart* (1946), *Chronicle*, and *Appalachian Spring*.

Graham said that the body is a sacred garment, our first and our last. In the Graham world dances are sacred because they are inextricably woven with our human bodies, the very vessels of life. In her 1963 interview with dance writer Walter Terry, Graham spoke of the moment of "finding yourself as a house in which your spirit lives."[3] To find oneself within it, one must first know the house. The house, garment, and vessel are metaphors in her work that take us to the essential and elemental (emotion as element) relationship of human being and spirit in the world. From the unadorned presentation of her early "woolens" work of *Lamentation* and *Heretic* to the regaled "Greek cycle" with *Phaedra* and *Clytemnestra* (1958) and back again to essential forms in *Acts of Light (1981)* and *Rite of Spring* (1984); these representations of the human body in space chronicle her life's perspective. Through physical and oral tradition, dancers experience Graham as an empowering philosopher/artist who created a body of work wherein the dancer stands revealed as the creator of each movement from the inside/out.

Known for her intense physicality, artistic integrity, and imagery, former principal dancer and co-Artistic Director Terese Capucilli speaks to this artistic process:[4]

There is that recognition of the miracle of a human being. There is the body and its memory. There is that passion and curiosity and driving force that the artist must have at all turns. There is the ability to plant a seed and have it grow internally in the individual but ultimately it is a selfless act .... There is absolutely that curiosity for life and its adventures and ultimately the acceptance process of the journey, that every road is a learning process. Every road leads in some way to a sense of self as an artist and a sense of freedom. All of these kinds of things are important in

[3] 92nd Street Y interview.
[4] Personal interview with Terese Capucilli.

terms of philosophies for living. Things I try to give my son. You are not always successful, right? There are a lot of things that happen that when you get to the bump in the road. You want to just like take a different road but it is getting over that bump. In so many ways, Martha's technique is similar, moving through her work those bumps are the places where you grow the most ... Sources of inspiration are really key ... how to bring yourself into what you do expressively.

Capucilli is renowned for her use of imagery in her roles both as performer and teacher. The time she spent working with Graham, having a master choreograph on her body (again, the sic-sensuous concept of writing a narrative upon another body) gave Capucilli a particular authority which is palpable when a dancer works with her in the studio. Capucilli continues:

Martha changed the way we look at dance. It is still circulating. That circulating feeling is making this incredible soup. It is not that the Graham dancers are over here and everybody else is over here. It is all integrated now but it requires everyone to stay the course in order for the incredible secrets and storytelling [to be revealed] and [to have] the ability to understand one another. That all comes from a sense of listening and sensitivity in the world. To those of us who have spoken Martha's language and are out there teaching it is important to continually invest in ways of bringing these philosophies [to bear], even if someone does not have the ability to be in a Graham class. As an artist I feel that sense of responsibility to try to smell the flowers. I see social media as a way of reaching someone in a sensitive beautiful way ... The reason I teach ... as a way to further showcase, in the static form, the immense sensitivity, empathy, humanity, and strength which are present in the energetic pathway, down the forearm and into the heel of the palm.

Dance that is formed through the sympathetic, feeling human body activates empathetic communication and open us to the possibility of compassionate response. Graham's dance language expresses archetypal phrases and gestures that are touchstones for its native speaker-movers. The following are some additional key movements of the language.

- Contraction (a curvilinear expansion of the spine and torso initiated from the breath).
- Release (lengthening that curve into space).
- Spiral (oppositional physicality that engages one direction of movement in contrast to another thus creating physical suspension and control of one's weight).
- Shift of weight (moving through space by consciously engaging the body with gravity).

FIGURE 7 Appalachian Spring. *Terese Capucilli, Mikhail Baryshnikov, Maxine Sherman, and Rudolf Nureyev. Photograph by Nan Melville.*

FIGURE 8 Lamentation. *Dancer: Pei-Ju Chien-Pott. Photograph by Christopher Jones.*

Active Emotion

People dance in order to connect, to heal, and to attempt to make sense of human being in the world. Dances are invaluable assets held and stored in our memory banks to be accessed for inspiration or solace. Our dances themselves are symbols whose meanings are renewed and redefined through performance of an informed and practiced dancing body. The phenomenological continuum of dance activates archetypes in performance such as joy, ritual, heroism; but also rage, jealousy, grief, and sacrifice. Historical modern dances such as those by Graham, José Limón, Alvin Ailey, Katherine Dunham, and others are deeply personal librettos of the body for both performers and audiences. A sic-sensuous interplay of dance arises here that casts the choreographer as author writing upon the body of the dancer. If you are lucky enough to dance a role Graham created for herself, such as *Lamentation* or *Frontier*, you are able to experience archetypal activation. When Graham danced *Lamentation* in 1930 without shame for exposing her emotional expression, she engaged the physical profundity of grief in her body's own language. The simple and raw nature of the *Lamentation* still provides us access, as audience or performer, to bear witness to the inherent dignity in human emotion. This is one reason I believe teaching repertory is vitally important to the continuation of the Martha Graham Dance Company. Through a marriage of will and form, repertory activates information that has been gathered and archived over generations of bodies. It is through physically experiencing these archetypes in movement that we are able to access those memories held deep within the flesh, bones, and blood.

An Ecology of Dance: The Studio

"A great piece of sculpture is never self-contained; it reaches out to affect the space around it. We exist in space that is the energy of the world, and each of us is a recipient of that energy, if he so wills."[5]

In the studio a dancer engages the entire ecology of the Graham world, lineage, and canon. Her philosophies are part and parcel of teaching the technique; learning the technique provides access to the power of her dances. Daily technique class presents the perfect forum for teachers to discuss Graham's philosophies while the dances themselves reveal the philosophical underpinnings which support them. The dancer puts intention into practice in the physical space and environment of the studio. Graham's use of space is

---

[5] ABC news interview with Martha Graham.

significant in her choreography. She asks the dancer to throw their body into space, tear into the space, alter the space with their energy and physicality. Graham asserted that it takes ten years to become a dancer.[6] I do not believe that it takes ten years to become a dancer. However, it does take time to develop one's inherent talents, physical power, and the extraordinary level of articulation for which Graham dancers are renowned.

One of the most quoted sources of Graham's philosophy on being a dancer, and also a beautiful piece of writing, is her essay "I Am a Dancer." It highlights Graham's insights into the effort, focus, and devotion necessary to create a life in dance in a society and culture such as the United States of America, which in the main does not support or value it. It is a call to action and a resource for inspiration once again for generations of dancers and movement practitioners. Graham writes:

> It takes about 10 years to make a mature dancer. The training is two-fold. First comes the study and practice of the craft which is the school where you are working in order to strengthen the muscular structure of the

FIGURE 9 *The company in creative process with choreographer Nacho Duato. Lloyd Knight (center) with Tadej Brdnik and Maurizio Nardi. Photograph by Blakeley White-McGuire.*

---

[6] See Peter Glushanok et al., *A Dancer's World.*

body. The body is shaped, disciplined, honored and, in time, trusted. The movement becomes clean, precise, eloquent, truthful. Movement never lies. It is a barometer telling the state of the soul's weather to all who can read it. This might be called the law of the dancer's life – the law which governs its outer aspects.[7]

Embedded Foundational Philosophies within the Technique and Dances[8]

The following synopses of embedded philosophies of Graham's theater and personal interviews from Graham-identifying artists are presented here for contemplation by the novice, practiced artist and audience member alike. These paraphrased philosophies[9] attributed to Graham have been repeated over decades in dance classes around the world as inspiration and sustenance.

1. "Stay aware of the urges that motivate you"

Then comes the cultivation of the being from which whatever you have to say comes. It doesn't just come out of nowhere it comes out of a great curiosity. The main thing of course is that there is only one of you in all time, just one and if that is not fulfilled then something has been lost. Ambition is not enough, necessity is everything. It is through this that the legends of the soul's journey are told with all their tragedy and bitterness and sweetness of living.

Sacrifices are a necessary part of a dancer's life. It is necessary to immerse in an actorly way, into character, history, and narrative of each work in order to understand and covey it with authority. In my own life a necessity to dance, not simply move but to dance, has been integral to my self-expression. Indeed the energy within a particular a dance requires total commitment to the cultivation of the spirit that enables anyone to stand upon the stage. Moving in the particular way that is *dancing* exercises my soul.

In the following interview, dancer Abdiel Jacobsen speaks about their[10] life in dance and the philosophies that motivate their work as artist and activist. A Ballroom Dance Champion and educator, Jacobsen was a principal dancer with the Martha Graham Dance Company from 2011–18. An advocate for gender equality, they are currently developing choreography for both contemporary and ballroom genres.

---

[7] Graham. *Blood Memory*.
[8] Attributed to Martha Graham.
[9] Each of these is paraphrased or specifically quoted from Graham's autobiography, *Blood Memory*.
[10] Jacobsen's preferred gender pronoun.

BWM   *Of Graham's philosophies, which resonate, sustain, and inspire you?*

AJ   *"There is only one of you that exists all of time. Because there is no duplicate of you, your expression is inherently unique. Therefore, it is your duty to share you authenticity with the world. If you do not it will be lost forever and the world will not have it, the world will never benefit from your gift." That pulled me through so much trauma and turmoil from my life, not just dance. When I was twenty-two, I came out to my family seven months after I moved to New York. I was dancing with Graham 2 and then got into the main company as an apprentice. I said "I need to be myself, I need to be authentic!" Graham was such a central part to how I moved through life and still is, not just in my career but in my life! Coming out, owning my truth, staying true to who I am and voicing it. We contribute to the world through our truth. So that quote really helped me come out.*

When I announced that I am gender fluid, it was a second coming out. I do not identify as solely male or female. I am a combination of both. I always felt that inside of me, and Graham again was someone who I went back to in that discovery. She states in that same passage, "Follow the urges that motivate you." That urge is what makes you who you are. That is your authenticity. That is what motivates you to keep getting up to say I want to create! I want to interact with the world! I feel urged to fully express my gender fluidity.

The second quote is from "I am a dancer." "Whether it is to practice dance by dancing or life by living the principles are the same." Particularly in Western societies, dance is often viewed as a commodity, an institutionalized package that is marketed and sold. That perspective isolates our all-encompassing connection to the world around us. Martha's words remind us that dance is not separate from who we are; dance is life. The practice of dancing teaches you the practice of life skills. Oh my gosh, when I hear that quote I feel so empowered to be a dancer. It is like "Martha Graham you make me feel like … I am a fucking dancer! I am life!" I know life because I understand discipline, perseverance, how to push past the precipice of what seems impossible and make it possible for myself. We do that as dancers. I can do anything that I put my mind to. We are otherworldly on such a divine platform. Graham's words make me feel that my life has such an enriching mission. Martha is a Queen!

Jacobsen continues sharing how Graham's philosophies continues to influence their work.

I continue to use Graham's philosophy and her technique in other expressions. Martha Graham left us an invaluable tool to utilize in crafting our artistic expression. Modern contemporary dance and Ballroom dance are such isolated worlds that most people on each side do not even know what the other is like. I am a rare case. As a practitioner and insider of both of those worlds, I found so many connections between them on a fundamental level. The shift of weight and the emphasis and carriage of the spine into how we move are such beautiful connections!

Jacobsen continues to describe their creative work in a variety of dance styles, infusing activism with their joy, passion, and love of dance.

My mission and my vision moving forward is to take these teachings and philosophies and unify them. That is what I am doing with Kristine [ballroom partner]. In 2019, we co-founded a multimedia production company, Trān-sēnd'Dæns, that takes pride in a constant never-ending platform for the unconventional, non-traditional artists and creative minds across the board to push forward ideas, projects, and visions that break barriers and transcend the standard of their time. Trān-sēnd'Dæns's mission is to serve the greater needs of humanity through collaborative efforts with various groups, individuals, and organizations in the world of creative and performing arts, entertainment, and healthcare industries. Our company seeks to reveal the emotional layout of the core of humanity by ushering our vision into the future while honoring the past.

Martha Graham said, "It takes ten years to make a dancer," and I understand there can be some problematic implications with that. Some people feel that is a condescending way of saying "well if you don't dance for that long, you are not worthy to teach it." However, I resonate with Martha's statement from my personal experience of studying her technique for ten years. I danced with the Company for seven years and studied it in college for three, so I literally got the ten-year culmination. It is so funny because right now talking about it I feel that after that ten-year period, finally I am ready to really unpack my voice. I have committed to that. I found so much value in committing to Graham's technique, her philosophies, and repertoire. And now I am able to utilize all of that experience to hone in on my own voice. Kristine and I are doing that right now with our choreography. Kristine told me, "You know she danced with Twyla [Tharp] and Twyla was obsessed with Martha." The lineage is all there.

Here Jacobsen embraces feminism not as a political act but as a way of understanding:

Of course it is not a coincidence for me [working with] all of these women. It is important for women to create work and tell stories especially in our society where women, particularly women of color, have been historically erased. It is a time for women and those who are challenging the binary and finding more depth and complexities in who we are as bodies and beings. This is a time to tap into that which is feminine. Woman is the divine creator. The world has been so overly masculine. We need to find balance and honor the divine feminine, which is all-encompassing and holistic, not just erect and linear. This is where we could go with Graham's legacy. I really hope people who come from Graham continue to expand her legacy.

There is another thing about Graham; those moments of stillness that are so energized. The energy of everyone in the space even when you are not highlighted, is still supporting everyone. That is the feminine, the sense of supporting everyone in the space. It is not just about the one person in the spotlight. Even in our stillness we all have to stay equally energized, fully present. That translates to everything you do.

2. "Work the body from the inside out—the courage to be vulnerable"[11]

Lamentation (1930) is the perfect example of Graham's enduring legacy in visual art, theater, and dance. In it she is exploring the deeply personal terrain of the inner landscape. A solitary woman sits rocking (shifting) side to side (rather than forward and back) on a bench. The direction of the movement is significant in that she is not rocking to comfort herself. She shifts side to side, the movement indicates a break from the natural. It demonstrates a resistance generated from the inside—the spirit struggling inside of its container. As Graham in her own words said, "the body stretches inside of its own skin." She places the dancer inside of a purple tube of stretch jersey fabric that is in a constant state of constriction, against which the dancer must push out.

Nearly a hundred years after its premier, *Lamentation* has become a ritual acknowledgment of the grief experienced during times of great loss. Its quiet struggle is an expression of the unutterable. It is the guttural wail of grief calling to mind Eduard Munch's painting *The Scream* in its intensity and simplicity of form. *Lamentation* is a prime example of modern art from the twentieth century. It is also emblematic of dance and the inner landscape innovating with textiles for ritual and healing which has been the role of dance throughout humanity.

Graham pitches the body forward with veiled eyes, hands at her sternum or solar plexus as if she is waiting in vain for relief. We as audience can imagine the feeling of being inside of the woman's body seeing the unborn baby or the child never conceived. To date, only women have performed *Lamentation* within the Company itself. This may change and perhaps should change, but for a time this dance revealed an experience that women know from the inside out—that of the barren womb and the instinctually cathartic cry that comes from deep within it. The physical revelation transforms

---

[11] This is a blending of ideas taken from teachings espoused in the studio and from *Blood Memory*.

that pain, grief, and loss into a beauty that provides an experience of a deep presence with one's humanity that transcends gender. In *Lamentation* we experience dance/theater as ritual medicine.

Katherine Crockett, former principal dancer and current performer and producer of her own Exquisite Muse Productions, speaks in her interview about looking into different facets of transcendent art:

The cycle of life and the empowerment of looking into one's own shadow and embracing it … When I dance about it I somehow transcend my own small personal self. That's why we see something on stage. Yuriko[12] said this—she was talking about the power of and the importance of making something universal. She said you know no one wants to see you on stage crying. You need to go do that somewhere else. We don't want to see you on stage crying, we want to see the cry. We want to see the thing itself. Because then we see ourselves in it, we see our cry.

So it doesn't mean if you're playing this character that cries that you're not putting your own personal experience into that, you have to do that as well. But then it can't stay there. It has to go to some other place where you let them in. I just feel like Martha Graham's work has the ability to give you, as the performer, this vehicle to put the most personal, intimate stuff into it but then transform it into something that is really universal. That is the power of art.

She continues to articulate how art transforms experience through catharsis:

Art has the ability to make you feel the pain but yet transcend that pain. You go through it and you are transcended by the experience of it. That's what performing her work is like, this amazing catharsis. It is visually stunning, architecturally stunning, the costumes … she wasn't just doing rote movement; she was collaborating with artists musicians [on] her whole vision of theater. It wasn't just about talented dancers. Her work, although abstract, has narrative, and there is a sense of the theatrical in it, which I love. I love embodying these different characters, even if they are in abstract situations. Embodying them for me was just as important as being able to dance well—you couldn't separate the two. You can't step out of the role to do a really awesome split jump and then get back in the role. The split jump either has to express what you're trying to say, or you're out of it. You're not demonstrating the beauty of your technique even in a piece that was completely about the demonstration of technique, which is one of her late pieces from 1981, Acts of Light, "Helios" section. When I performed it, I never felt like I was demonstrating the technique. I felt like I was going through a ritual, which was this deep physical work of offering the body, of this movement that was so … reaching out as far as you can

---

[12] Yuriko Kikuchi.

go and pulling in with the group of people in the circle and ending in a gesture of offering.

Relating to cycles and gestures of offering we hear again from rising star Leslie Andrea Williams. It is this cycle of sharing the work, generation after generation, that provided the connection for Williams to see her own potential within the canon and eventually win a role in the Company. This example illuminates the significance of continuing to share the work in both practice and theory.

Developing a role is about the constant study but also understanding life. The more you live life, have your experiences, it really helps to inform your work in Graham. I guess for most artists but especially because [Graham] is so much about human experience. There is no other choice but to look inside and understand on a deep level how you feel and think.
… Also I think that I understood what it meant to be a part of the lineage mostly when I joined the Company because I realized that there is such a large history involved. Not only with Martha but with the dancers who were in her company and worked with her and how that all was passed down generationally. When I joined the Company, I felt like I had a lot of natural ability and I attest that to Terese because for her Graham was emotion, more than technique almost. Terese felt like two years of Graham was not enough and she would say, "I don't have much time to give you the information so I really want you to understand the emotion"—the sensory images. Imagery is so important to the work. I felt like I really understood that by doing the technique.[13]

3. "You are in competition with one person only, the person you know you can become"[14]

Graham's choreography for *Errand into the Maze* (1947) provides a way of becoming who one is capable of being through its demanding rigor. A duet between a man (the Creature of Fear) and a woman (Ariadne), this dance is a ritual performance of overcoming fear: the fear of stepping out on one's own and the fear of activating one's sexual power. It is also about the destructive and/or generative power of the mind. Through its hyper-expressive physicality and symbolism, this powerful dance develops the performers inner strength to go forward into life's inevitable next steps.

Errand into the Maze begins with the drama of a first step as the woman commences her journey into a labyrinth. She moves out into a strange landscape, and immediately the Creature of Fear appears. There is no turning

---

[13] Personal interview with Leslie Andrea Williams.
[14] Peter Glushanok et al., *A Dancer's World*.

back, only to go forward into the challenge of facing her fears. Graham's use of space and sculpture are integral to her aesthetic presentation here. Stage settings such as Noguchi's famous standing pelvic bone and long rope spread out upon the stage indicate a pathway and illuminate Graham's appreciation of the body in space; the moving body as the center of the stage.

When I performed as the protagonist Ariadne, I physically felt my imagination open up. In the beginning of the dance Ariadne steps away from but quickly returns to her starting place three times before entering into the labyrinth. Despite her conquering of the Creature of Fear, Ariadne knows that fear will inevitably return even as she steps out of her darkness and into the light. *Errand* contains moments of battle for which Graham's technique gives you the tools to win. Graham's choreography always presents physical moments of true struggle and uncertainty as opportunities to access one's personal will power.

As one of Graham's greatest interpreters, particularly in *Errand Into The Maze* Christine Dakin has influenced generations of dancers internationally. A creative artist and master teacher in her own right, Dakin spoke with me about her view on the role of the artist today:

Any great art, great artist has that path. You can find that path through any kind of art. It is a way to relate yourself to the world, to what you do and why you do it. There are as many ways of doing that as there are artists. But they all have certain things in common. It is not surprising that, for my way of looking at it, that many of Martha's dances thematically were about the individual confronting the group. I do not think it is an accident that many, many artists have gone the Rite of Spring *route. That is, the genetic human characteristic to locate the outsider, to create a relationship with the outsider, either as the outsider or acting on the outsider. I think that is something that Martha was concerned about. The artist is not there to entertain you. The artist's work is different, and how the artist fits into society is very complicated, very varied, but it's different. It is a different series of tasks and responsibilities in a way, and it is easily misunderstood.*[15]

This is why becoming the one you know you are capable of becoming, individualism, is so valuable to society. Dakin continues:

There are some people who take it on themselves as a personal challenge and do not allow or expect themselves to have anything to do with the outside world. You are in competition with nobody but yourself, the person that you can become. Okay, that is fine but you are living in the world. So if you want to live in the world, how do you maintain your way, your understanding, your experience—how do you keep the world from having an impact on you? You cannot; very few people can. So that place where the individual butts up against society is a dangerous and fraught place. We see it now in the culture: me, me, me, selfies, myself and buying.

---

[15] See Dakin interview.

All of that has nothing to do with anything that I recognize as being a constructive or rewarding way to look at the relationship of an individual to a society. So the artist being completely unique has to negotiate that confrontation with society in the same way that any individual does but with a lot more baggage that you have to take along.[16]

4. "The dance is a fever chart of the heart telling the weather of one's soul to all who can read it"[17]

In the following excerpt from Walter Terry's 1963 interview with Graham at the 92nd Street Y, she speaks to understanding oneself and uncovering one's personal truth.

WT *Why did you give a universal core to the heroines that have come from history, from the past? Why is it that you had a concern with the figures from Greece, why Greece particularly? You as an American dancer.*

MG *There seems to be a way of going through in Greek literature and Greek history. All of the anguish, all of the terror, all of the evil and arriving someplace. In other words, it is the instant that we all look for, the catharsis through the tragic happenings. Everyone in life has tragic happenings. Everyone has been a Medea at some time or another. That doesn't mean you killed your husband or that you've killed your children. But in some deep way the impulse has been there to cast a spell, to use every ounce of your power. And that's true for a man as well as the woman ... You have to look for the truth. You eat the truth in your mouth. Sometimes it is bitter and sometimes sweet, but you have to eat life. Everyone needs to savor the hidden room inside himself. There are some things you cannot teach—either they are there or not. If you are going to grow, you have to absorb life. You have to take experience inside your body.*[18]

Knowing one's own truth leads to the confidence, fortitude, and tenacity to tell one's own story or express a point of view through the lens of art. Any person who, as Graham said, "walks the high wire of circumstance,"[19] understands the moment of recognition of mortality, vulnerability, and potential for destruction, especially where romance and possession take hold. In her dance about possessive jealousy, *Cave of the Heart*, Graham's message seems to be from a woman to women: beware of the destructive power of jealousy.

---

[16] See Dakin interview.
[17] Graham, *Blood Memory*.
[18] 1968 Interview for the 92nd Street Y between Martha Graham and Walter Terry.
[19] From Graham's essay, *I Am A Dancer*.

Interpreting those female roles that Graham created as a showcase for herself demands a dancer's extreme focus on research, imagination, and physicality. This is the role of repertory. Its inherently rigorous process of discovery serves as a catalyst for both stretch and surrender to the profound experience of inhabiting a life/dance that has been energetically carved out by others. These have been invigorating and challenging (in the best ways) for me and were a large part of my work in the Company. Death/ re-birth, when I dance, even when I step into a great historic role, I am always Blakeley. I am not transformed into Medea but through an alchemy of energies, a transformation occurs that illumines the archetype of Medea.

In her retelling of the Greek myth of Medea, Graham renders the corrosive effects of jealousy through four characters: Medea, Jason, the Princess, and the Chorus. Jason flaunts his young princess in front of Medea. We feel her humiliation, the pain in her heart through full-bodied convulsions, waling lunges, and a series of pitch turns that Graham choreographs into her retelling. The Chorus, in her pleading knee crawls, sees that destruction is mounting and tries to press Medea back where she began the dance; into the Noguchi serpent heart set piece coiled on the ground. When Medea finally poisons the Princess, Jason is also destroyed as he embraces his new love in her suffering. Medea transforms into a serpent in her treacherous triumph. She is doomed to remain in her serpent cage indefinitely as expressed in the never-ending knee vibrations she performs until the curtain drops. Placing Medea in the prison/ sculpture of the serpent and the sun, Graham and Noguchi as collaborators in Graham's retelling, show the duality of this archetype. On one hand, she is queen in her home, empowering herself to express her innermost desires in the face of Jason's cruelty and lack of compassion for her, but her indulgence in jealousy dooms her to a prison in her own heart.

5. "The dancer does what the body is capable of doing; they become in some arena an athlete of god"

To dance the lead in a Graham ballet is to inhabit a world, proceed through a journey, and experience raw emotion, generally from a female perspective. Discipline and repetition are springboards for spontaneity that can reveal the inner lives of characters. Technique can advance an individual dancer both in strength and tenacity. Implicit in a Graham dancer's physical strength is an inner flexibility and extreme range of control from deep inside the flesh. We acquire spiritual acumen that enables us to exercise our souls and to embody the legends of humanity.

One of the more rigorous of these dances in active repertory is *Chronicle*. Originally five sections, it is "a work of women working together"[20] that brings to life a feeling of the implacable specter of war while simultaneously

[20] Attributed to Dana Mills in a personal communication.

suggesting an alternative. It showcases the spirit of survival and highlights both visionary leadership and a willingness to be led in a new direction. Rather than using our bodies to dominate, the dance presents a possibility of cultivating the body in its highest and most powerful potential for beauty.

After a long absence from the Company's repertoire, *Chronicle* was reconstructed in 1994. Thanks to the preservation of a 1935 film by Julien Bryan, three out of the five original sections, *Spectre-1914*, *Steps in the Streets*, and *Prelude to Action*, were reimagined and, to a degree, recaptured. The process of reconstruction was recently documented in an article for *Dance Research Journal* by Professor Kim Jones of the University of North Carolina at Charlotte. In the article, Jones provides significant documentation of the actors in this reconstruction:

> ... *Prelude to Action*, was reconstructed in 1994 by original 1930s Graham dancer Sophie Maslow, and assisted by principal dancer Terese Capucilli, Rehearsal Director Carol Fried (Cowen), and Associate Artistic Director Diane Gray using film from Julien Bryan and photographs by Morgan. Primarily, Capucilli reconstructed the Graham solo in this section and the group reconstruction was led by Maslow. *Steps in the Street* was reconstructed by Yuriko Kikuchi, known professionally as Yuriko, former principal dancer with the Martha Graham Company (1944–1967) (Capucilli, e-mail message to author, May 10, 2015). Bryan, a photographer and documentary filmmaker, was a colleague of Willard and Barbara Morgan who introduced the Morgans to Martha Graham. Bryan filmed some of Graham's rehearsals in 1935. It is these films which were used in future reconstructions.[21]

In the reconstructed dance, the soloist in *Spectre-1914* wears an oversized black skirt heavily lined with blood red innards. The solo demands an intensity akin to a tsunami coming out of an ocean; even entering the stage requires a particular intensity. As the curtain rises or as the lights come up, it is imperative for the soloist to increase their physical presence. This kind of presence is not simply performing, but rather it is being intensity—the very thing itself, like the unstoppable force of a wave or a political movement. To perform in a ballet that places the female in the role of both carrier of devastation and empowered responder to that devastation is to transform oneself from the quotidian to the heroic. The demands on the physical body require spiritual intercession. It is at this nexus that performance and reality skew because although the performer is aware that no immanent danger exists, there is a real-time awareness that to stop in the middle of performance would mean metaphoric death. The dance is an energetic world; the urgency to life that is present during performance is authentically

---

[21] Kim Jones, "American Modernism: Reimagining Martha Graham's Lost Imperial Gesture (1935)."

related to an existential survival. I have personally experienced an inner monologue in performance that went something like this: *I may die here. I may evaporate into the ether beneath these burning lights.* This statement is not intended to be hyperbole.

The all-female cast is put through a grueling routine of continuous, rhythmic jumps and torqued shapes evocative of both personal isolation and unity within a group. It exemplifies the fortifying value of engaging in a physical act of performance. The opportunities for growth through *Chronicle* in terms of developing physical stamina and spirituality in community are enormous, it is a galvanizing dance. From the extreme athleticism of the split leap sits into a dynamic contraction to the floor and the double attitude jumps flying through the air in a circling *menege*, to the backwards walking entrance onstage in *Steps in the Street*, there are many physical challenges at every stage of this dance.

The existential realities experienced while performing repertory take form in many ways including narrative and abstracted story telling. During our 2019 interview, former principal dancer Elizabeth Auclair and I discussed her experiences performing some of Graham's leading roles, as well as her ideas around narrative versus abstraction in dance:

EA *The two pieces we have talked about,* Lamentation *and* Chronicle, *are much more abstract, although one could experience* Lamentation *as less abstract.*

BWM *I remember once in Italy watching you perform outside. You were dancing* Spectre *and I was just in awe.*

EA *The other pieces that I would mention that were very impactful upon me were the Greek works: Errand into the Maze, Night Journey, Jocasta, and also the role of Medea in Cave of the Heart. These are more plot driven, have a storyline—a structure that you hang everything on and work around, the way a vine weaves itself around a trellis. It is there and you work around and through it.*

I also think that we are storytellers whether we mean to be or not. We are meaning-seeking beings—we look for meaning in things. Even in abstract things, we say "what do you make of that?" You dance, you live through it, you bring it to life, and that is the storytelling. It is simply revealing a story.

With these three, Errand into the Maze, Cave of the Heart, *and* Night Journey, *the central character is reaching these very extreme places of emotional existence—these really extreme feeling states. There is fear on the edge of destruction; there is murderous rage and jealousy and there is absolute utter despair, and tragedy and trauma that does ruin, is ruinous. And that was the challenge. It is a really exciting process. The movement, the choreography itself, as in most of Martha's work, evokes the feeling state that the character is meant to be embodying. And that goes so far into bringing you into the character. You become the story through the movement, which brings the character to the place they need to be. In this way, artifice or "acting" is not necessary; if one goes deeply and truly into the movement—through the movement into the character—it's all there.*

BWM   *Talking about roles, which were the most impactful upon you as a performer?*

EA   Lamentation *is such a deep and subtle endeavor into a kind of multipart, multifaceted exploration of this feeling state but also of the power of shape and design to both reflect and imbue the sense, the essence of the feeling and the state of the being—that grief, and pain, and sorrow.* Lamentation *was a never-ending journey of exploration. I loved it, the subtlety of it.*

Also the lead in Chronicle, *for very different reasons. It was much more of a broad, impacting and powerful kind of role. It demanded a lot, and went through a whole trajectory of experience, as does* Lamentation, *but in a different way. I didn't see it as a character but as a representation of something much larger, a conceptual identity: the ghost of war. It becomes an abstraction. It was amazing to try to embody that.*

EA   *Yes, there is something in that when it is not the character of a person. It is this abstract projection of a whole pallor—in this case the specter of war. All of the different components of that—the exploration is so fascinating.*

In some dances Graham created a new world. In *Dark Meadow* (1946) she opened imaginative spaces in the mind through her choreographic terrain of archetypal imagery. Principal dancer Miki Orihara, who danced many of Graham's roles speaks to this idea though the lens of Japanese cultural influences in *Dark Meadow*:

MO   *There is something like a pilot light, something in her that was always a small fire that could make her switch on. It is an interesting thing for me because I am Japanese. She … always had Japanese dancers. I remember talking to her in the hallway sitting on the bench waiting for her car. She would talk to me about why she liked Japanese philosophy and culture—that was so interesting.*

BWM   *What was it about Japanese culture, philosophy, and aesthetics?*

MO   *Certain things I do not think that I can explain. Asia is big but … thinking about China, Korea, Japan we have temples and shrines … in Japan mostly there is nothing decorative. Everything is naturalistic, like Isamu Noguchi's ideas. We use the rock and we are not going to turn the* *rock into something else but are going to use the rock's heart in the art. That way you give respect to the rock and the rock can speak a little bit of its own. That kind of idea.*

There is a word in Japan, I do not have an English translation. It means 'quiet beauty speaks loudly.' It is that kind of idea. Culturally we have that. I think from Western eyes it is very different, maybe that is why she was attracted to that too.

BWM *She is often quoted saying things like "the body is a sacred garment." Do you see a connection in that to Japanese culture?*

MO *Yes. I think it is that teaching of Zen. Yuriko always talked about Martha being very much interested in Zen. The monk Suzuki was in the US, and many Americans read his book. I think that is when [Graham] choreographed Dark Meadow. Of course Freud and Jungian psychology were influential too, but the* Dark Meadow *sets were reflective of a Japanese temple. The stone garden—it becomes harmony, a universe it becomes one place. I was surprised to hear about her Japanese [affinity] because she was raised in California, where there is so much Chinese influence.*

Orihara's words articulate the multicultural influences inherent in Graham's canon, which amplifies the significance of our one shared humanity. For an outside observer or brief visitor to the canon, its rigorous devotion to philosophy and specific practices can be misinterpreted as dogmatic. What interests me, however, is the laser-sharp focus needed to achieve proficiency in its performance. The work lives beyond the personality of one director/ teacher or another. Its labor resides in the thoughtful development of character, technique, art, and deep emotional expression. Her philosophies for shaping and caring for the body enhance the spiritual aspect of Graham's work and the dances themselves create a map leading to a vital life of the body, mind, and spirit through the body as instrument, movement as medium.

3

Technique/Symbols: Teaching and Learning through the Female Form

She created a movement idiom that had within it inherent points of departure for meaning.

—*Mary Hinkson*[1]

Dancers train in order to "keep the channel open"[2] to the deepening meanings of gesture, rhythm, and phrases of movements revealed through the body. Throughout her life's-long excavation of movement coming from her own body, Graham revealed her new interpretations of accepted stories and myths. Although she was not overt in expressing herself as a feminist Graham's body of work reveals the inherent power of female physicality through simply dancing it. She did not need to explain it, she danced it. The numinous affects of art are present when the unconscious made is conscious.[3]

In this chapter we explore Graham's work through the lens of a female artist working in the early, mid-, and late twentieth century inside of a patriarchal society. The historic time frame of her life made her work a transgressive act that influenced the physical and psychological shape of her dances. Because Graham mined her life for inspiration, she inevitably addressed themes of sexual repression and sexual liberation. Her body was the laboratory where she experimented with form, breath, and blood memory. Consciously or not, any student of her canon is dancing an epistemology of radical feminism and transformation.

---

[1] *Dance Magazine, Special Issue: Martha Graham*, July 1991: 44.
[2] Quote from Martha Graham's letter to Agnes De Mille.
[3] Carl Jung, "Until you make the unconscious conscious, it will direct your life and you will call it fate."

FIGURE 10 Spectre-1914. *Dancer: Blakeley White-McGuire. Photograph by Guilherme Licurgo.*

In *Night Journey* (1947), for example, Graham exposes inner desires, curiosities, and fears as she reframes the myth of Oedipus Rex through the eyes of Queen Jocasta. The dance begins at the moment just before the queen's suicide. Graham retrogrades the story to show the audience how Jocasta arrived to her death: through willful blindness. The chorus also known as the Daughters of the Night heave, stamp, and jump[4] as they implore Jocasta to reconsider her intentions. Overriding her instincts, she

---

[4] See the photograph on the cover of this book.

gives in to the passion that would end in ruin for both herself and her son/ lover, Oedipus. Guttural contractions and leg extensions pulled up from the ground through her womb symbolize not only the birth of Jocasta's son but also the ripping apart of her own self for the sake of surrendering to passion. Graham's technique serves to convey this very peculiar drama. The dance is quintessential Graham in terms of dance technique. Her knee work in the seduction scene duet, for example, uses archaic form to accentuate the female hips at this moment. When I danced this role with my partner Lorenzo Pagano as Oedipus, I was struck by how organically Graham's technique facilitated the rising up from the kneeling position. Exercises such as the zig-zag pleading primes the dancer's core (center abdominal muscles) for rising up from the floor and strengthen their physical presence through the use of the back in spiral.

At the end of the dance, after the couple have consummated their bond and triggered the revelation of their true connection (as mother and son), Oedipus blinds himself. Yet, he continues to live. Jocasta returns to her rope which has remained on stage since the opening scene. She takes the rope, her umbilical cord from the beginning of the dance, in her hands and ends her life in the final scene. As the curtain lowers, Tiresias, the blind seer (oracle) takes his last walks across the stage as if speaking to the inevitability of the ancient story and the inherent futility of trying to avoid one's destiny.

One must become who one is. —Martha Graham

Since its premier, Graham's retelling of *Oedipus Rex* via *Night Journey* has been a springboard for thought around cultural norms and sexual mores. In 2019, New York City-based choreographer Netta Yerushalmy created a choreographic intervention titled *Paramodernities* through which she deconstructed and reimagined several modern dance masterworks. *Night Journey* was one of these. Using her personal choreographic methodologies, Yerushalmy challenged how meaning is attributed, constructed, and disrupted within cherished structures of iconic and revered dances from the modern canon. In keeping with the content-driven traditions of both the Graham and modern dance more broadly, *Paramodernities* challenged audiences to open themselves to the sensation of things as they are perceived in real time, not as they are known historically.

Through Yerushalmy's deconstruction of cultural memory and choreographic habits, she opened a new potential for developing differing lenses through which to view the modern dance legacy. Her take on Graham's *Night Journey* titled *Paramodernities #2/Trauma, Interdiction, and Agency In "The House Of The Pelvic Truth"* was also addressed in an essay by scholar Carol Ockman who acknowledges the potency of Graham's feminist explorations. The following is excerpted from the introduction of Ockman's essay:

FIGURE 11 *Lorenzo Pagano and Blakeley White-McGuire reclining on a Noguchi set piece in* Night Journey. *Photograph by Christopher Jones.*

My exploration of *Night Journey* begins in a dental chair with a personal, if small, tale of bodily trauma. As I underwent oral surgery, I realized that I was reclining at the same angle as Noguchi's bed for Jocasta and Oedipus.

Ockman continue with an analysis of ideas embedded in the dance:

Along with physical and emotional trauma, central themes in my essay are Graham's woman-centered world (the "House of Pelvic Truth," the "vaginal cry") and its subversion of traditional male narratives—shifting the focus to a female protagonist, using symbolic spaces to explore the female psyche, the universal psyche interpreted by Freud, Jung, and others, as well as Graham's and Jocasta's inner feelings.

I also talk about what Netta [Yerushalmy] is doing with Graham and the ways in which the eroticism and female-centeredness of Graham's work anticipate Second Wave Feminism by twenty years. Her [Graham] bloodthirsty repertory, her bad girls or anti-heroines who defy expectations much as she did, not only make *Night Journey* relevant today but also help us consider questions central to representation now.

Ockman brings the reader to the role of art itself through the lens of Yerushalmy's intervention with Graham:

The rigorous distillation of form *a la Graham* and *a la Yerushalmy* opens veins of deep emotion and shocks us into thought. What does it mean to create work that exposes the body's discord? To give form to psychic trauma through the wordless language of the body? Can it make us see, feel, even do what we might not otherwise?

Engaging with Ockman's analysis supports my assertion that, intentionally or not, Graham was making feminist art. Indeed, some seventy years after its creation, *Night Journey* is still inspiring women to assess the inherent trauma of birth and repressed desire. Graham reconfigured archetypal myths, historically presented from the patriarchal perspective, in her own female voice, thus projecting woman onto the stage as human beyond the object of someone else's desire—she is a player in her own destiny. Tragedies such as *Oedipus Rex* teach us that sometimes there is no reason, there is no "out," and we must simply live a situation through to its end.

Graham's technique provides a method for all dancers, regardless of their gender, to develop their bodily strength and articulate the desires of the flesh through a subjective physical self-investigation. Through its inherent care for and celebration of the body, her technique holds tremendous agency for the empowerment of all people in the face of cultural objectification found in social norms, advertising, and socio-economic politics. I could not find a specific reference to any statement by Graham addressing gender significance or feminism. Furthermore, several of the dancers whom I interviewed for this book and who worked with Graham personally did not see, attribute, or express any gendered significance to the technique. However, the action of women teaching men about expressive physicality and ways of moving coming from the female anatomy, chemistry, psyche does provide male-identifying and non-binary identifying people entry to explore their anatomy, chemistry, and psyche outside of dominant patriarchal culture. It is significant!

Unlike classical European ballet wherein historically, the female body was primarily objectified as a form to be shaped into perfection (from aesthetics of monarchy); Graham technique developed from a starting point of woman as subject and through her aesthetic lens. This is not to place value on any gender over another. It is rather, simply, to highlight the extant potential for diversity in physical information. The work of the Martha Graham Dance Company and school continues to influence dancers of all gender identities. By providing vital information about the potential within the human body and imaginations regardless of sexual orientation or gender identification, each dancer may activate our own innate vitality. This is why we dance it and why we must dance it. We hear again from dancer/activist Abdiel Jacobsen:

BWM *Speaking to your work with the Martha Graham Dance Company do you connect with the idea of the technique coming from a female body? In contrast to codified dance forms that in a heteronormative patriarchal society were typically placed upon female bodies but also on male bodies— forcing male bodies into certain roles as well.*

AJ *I just made a public statement that my gender identity is gender fluid and my gender pronouns are they/them plural. That was literally two weeks ago. In unpacking all of that, I wrote a blog called awalkinmyheels. com [https //www.justabdiel.com/blog]. I started it five years ago. It was all about the discovery of my fluid nature as a person and specifically as a cis[5] man. I was really exploring then because I had such an attraction to feminine energy, feminine expression, woman, the female body physically. All of that went explicitly to this exploration of high heels as an apparatus.*

It really was a life-changing moment for me circling back to that after five years. Reflecting on that moment of self-questioning [and] coming to where I am now; finally being able to express myself in a dance form [Latin Ballroom] that is traditionally a heteronormative patriarchal superimposed way of dancing [gender] roles. I finally was able to dance it not from that perspective but I danced it from my own feeling!

Highlighting the significant of authentic action coming from the inside/out they explain the personal impact of community acknowledgment.

It was the first time being allowed to do that with the rule change [and] the first time ever I was competing in high heels. My aesthetic was fluid. I was competing in high heels wearing both the traditional male and female looks. The costuming, make-up, swapping roles in leadership [we][6] were able to ebb and flow with the call and the response, the supporter and the supported. [We were] able to flow through those dualities and really become one entity. I have chills even speaking it out to you because it was such a breaking through moment that allowed me to see "this is actually who I have always been, this is who I am and this is where I sit in my core as a whole" verses [being] divided.

Circling back to your question of Martha Graham and the female form, I resonate fully with the notion that it was created by a cis woman on a woman's body and that inherently has a connection to the feminine energy. I do believe that there are masculine and feminine energies. Some are more dominant than others. Some like me are in a more balanced state internally but outside forces pull us away from that balance. Personally that was such an important part of my life going to Martha Graham.

Jacobsen continues their activism by sharing personal experiences of transgressing societal norms with their readers and viewers in performances beyond the stage.

In my blog I wrote my whole journey of my attraction to womanhood, femininity, feminine energy, and female form. My whole life I have been connected to that. The way I unpacked it was first of all, my mother. My

---

[5] A person whose gender identity matches their sex assigned at birth.
[6] Jacobsen's dance female identifying dance partner Christine Bendul.

*mother was the first person who introduced me to dance. That is important
because the way she moves and moved as a cis woman very grounded in her
womanhood was empowering to me as a person. I was so drawn into my
mom's ability to connect to her power, her fluidity, her sensuality, her sense
of expression through her body. That was huge for me! I was always closer
to my mom … My mom accentuating all of her assets and her feminine
expression which she was so tied to. I observed this throughout my life.*

*Finally, when I was introduced to dance I realized that anything
I gravitated to was rooted in women's expression. Their physical
expression of movement through their bodies. It is no coincidence that
my grandmother, my mom's mother, started an all female troupe in the
Ivory Coast for over twenty years. They performed all over the country.
My mom's maiden name is Zuzuwa and the tribe is Bété. So I went to dig
deeper, what is Bété and what is my family, what are they known for? I
remember my mom telling us these stories about the Bété women. She said
that the Bété women were known for fighting in the war of Colonialism
against the French capturing their husbands. I heard my mom say, "I am
femme Bété," and she would say it like I am not someone to be messed
with, we fought in the war, freed our husbands in the war from capture. So
it is no coincidence that this idea of power and confidence and command
comes from the female form, the female essence, feminine energy. It is in
my cells. I believe in a cellular connection. Our ancestors passed trauma,
passed experiences, passed knowledge through the body so I have a
cellular connection to that experience. And my mom passed it on through
her demonstration in the household, with us in our home.*

As to how modern dance has influenced their path Jacobsen shares their
passion for the Graham technique of dance.

*Then I go and discover Martha Graham. It is not a coincidence that
after studying Lester Horton (from a man) and Paul Taylor (from a man)
I was not attracted to them. I definitely was attracted to Dunham.[7] I was
attracted to Dunham and Graham but for me Graham was it. When I
discovered Graham I felt that power. I did not make the connections at
that moment. I was not conscious of it but it was subconscious. I knew
this was where I needed to be because it felt like home. I believe someone
like me who is gender fluid, who connects to both essences both forms
and [with] my experience would be drawn to a cis woman who created
her technique for her body, on her body for women. Her company was all
women in the beginning. That was her perspective and I love it.*

*What I love about Martha Graham's technique is that it is not gendered.
Everyone learns the combinations the same. There is not a female variation
or a male variation like in Euro-centric classical dance traditions; there*

---

[7] Katherine Dunham was a celebrated choreographer, dancer, and anthropologist (1909–2006).

is no gender. That was my "a-ha" moment because for me coming from ballroom—it was ultra-gendered! I could not express my feminine side at that time because I had to play the heteronormative, patriarchal perspective of a man. So learning Graham technique was my next a-ha moment. I was like "wow, I can embrace my femininity, my womanhood and my power all in one and still be socially accepted." It was awesome!

They continue with critique and ideas of possibilities for future development.

However, the one caveat for me is the technique verses the repertory. That is the unfortunate thing. I always remember you [BWM] saying in one of your interviews that we [the Company at that time] did not know Martha Graham personally but we have her philosophy and her legacy. So we take that. I do not know [for certain] but I feel from her philosophy that she would want it to evolve. That is what she said to her dancers, she would never want her dancers to dance her role like she did.

The way I see Graham is that it is an evolving form and at this time and age the repertoire should represent where we are evolving as a collective consciousness on gender. I hope that the Company will keep Martha Graham's evolutionary, revolutionary spirit and realize that a lot of these ballets could be gender fluid for sure. Lamentation, Heretic, all of these early ballets that were more archetypal human emotion were negating gender. I hope they will open that door to have men and women experience those roles more. The first repertory I learned at the Graham School was Steps in the Street in 2010—that was my introduction to the Graham Center. I was the only man with the women, but that was what I was drawn to, that for me was Graham. That power!

I always felt more connected to that [female power roles] than the male/female gendered roles in Graham's ballets, the ones which came later when men joined the Company. I felt that I had to play the heteronormative role unfortunately. I have to be honest, getting those comments like "you need to dance like a man, you need to play the role of the hero and the hero is big chested and muscular ..."—these tropes of heteronormative patriarchy which did not align with who I was inside [indicates disappointment]. But I still played those roles as an actor. I was fine to play those roles because the technique that those roles were rooted in was still central to the character and the expression of the character and the movement. So there was a fine line of being true to who I was and balancing these heteronormative tropes, which were not who I was. But it was okay because of the technique was where it was rooted and that had no boundaries.

Speaking to the universality of dance and within Graham technique in particular Jacobsen digs into his roots in Africa.

BWM   I am interested in this idea of you feeling "at home" in the technique. What felt like home in the technique?

AJ *You know I was just speaking with Nya [Bowman][8] about this, and she was saying that when she first learned about Martha Graham she did not know that she was "White." She thought Graham was a "Black" woman and I get that. I am not "Black" American, I am African. I was born in Africa and raised by an African immigrant in America, so I have a direct link to my African heritage and culture, which is important for my perspective. My way of referencing dance comes directly from that tradition. I am very conscious of that. I grew up with traditional and contemporary West African dance and music, I was exposed to that community. With that said, I can say that [Graham] felt like home because those traditional West African dances are so grounded, barefooted, and there is a lot of articulation of the spine. All of the undulation and contraction and release, all of these things are so rooted in these indigenous, tribal dance forms and I was exposed to that as a kid, that was my first learning.*

That is why it feels like home because in Graham technique we are in touch with floor, our stance is widening, we are expanding, and we are focusing on our spine. That axis of the pelvis and the spine is very connected with African traditions. I know that she was into the raw electric way of expressing movement and getting into our animal nature. We always get these beautiful images and metaphors like the cobra, the condor, the eagle, these animals. In a lot of West African dance traditions, the movements are based off of animals, the crane and the serpent, etc. The animist energies of the earth, the animals and emulating those as forms of dance expression—movement expression. [Animists] are vegan; they do not eat animals, they commune with them and worship the spirit and the energies in the trees and the plants.

These are the conversations that I always wanted to have about Graham! It is so important. I think that is what she was going for, she wanted to transcend barriers of how the body should be perceived. For her to get to that place of transcendence she had to go back to that place of rawness. I believe she did. I connect to that. That is what feels like home for me. Going back to that rooted, grounded, visceral, animal, electric energy that is rooted in the pelvis and in the spine. The expansive nature of the body, I think that is connected to my heritage as an African. It is even more transcendent that Graham did not study these things [African dance] because it just shows how connected and universal the language of the body is. When you tap into that raw electric thing it just comes out. I want to make more direct bridges and I think there is a link to be made here.

As artists, our richest source of insight is our deepest personal experience.
—Lise Brody[9]

---

[8] Former Graham dancer living in Barcelona, Spain.
[9] My graduate school professor from Goddard College.

Using the body as instrument and movement as medium, Graham's dance language became a container for her own self-knowledge while simultaneously revealing the expressive potential of the universal[10] human body. She did this not by colonizing others' bodies, but by sharing her way of discovery with those dancers who came to her. For generations dancers have come to her house of the pelvic truth for training. To my knowledge no one is forced to be a Graham dancer; that road is taken of one's free will. As a dancing body in the world-at-large, Graham revealed the oppressed gender, the second sex, and transgressed traditional roles by activating personal authority over her body. From the beautifully developed floor work to the deep engagement of both the contraction and release these life-giving movements are initiated from the dancer's breath.

Many men have made significant contributions to the creation and continuity of the technique as well and still do. At the center of the heart of the Graham universe, however, are certain sensations, such as the contraction and release, which are inextricably tied to the female sexual center. The physiological idea of contraction in Graham's vernacular is expansion. This contraction is in contrast or even opposition to the default definition of contraction from the Merriam-Webster Dictionary where it is defined as "the shortening and thickening of a functioning muscle or muscle fiber." The action of a Graham contraction creates expansion and an opening within the body bringing the action birth to the dancing body-mind. The release from the shaping of the contraction is also an action on this continuum of expansion.

I believe that practicing Graham technique not only empowers women to fully explore and embody the power of their own biology, it does the same for men and other identifying persons who practice it as well. Harnessing ever-present tension into creative energy, these movements teach us all about the expansiveness of creativity and sex. Practicing Martha Graham's technique of dancing definitely teaches us about sex.

The cycle of life is present at all times in a dance studio. One is always coming into their strength while the other is acquiescing it. Graham developed her dance language over time and allowed it to change for the purpose of building choreographies that were rooted in the modern era for her contemporary expression. She began with all women then, as men entered her company, different physical strengths were incorporated including partnering. These contributions set a pattern for future development. After her physicality diminished, Graham began to use younger bodies from the ever-reliable generations of new dancers.

---

[10] I am sensitive to the problematics of the descriptor "universal" as it relates to cultural erasure. Here, I intend it use as an opening for conversation around the question "what is it to be human outside of cultural frames?" The phenomenological practice that prompts this inquiry is that of assimilation and reconstruction of familial lineage in a nation built upon Colonialism, such as the United States' American culture.

Hearing from the dancers themselves about the significance of "Martha's house" provides the reader with insights into the depth of thought and feeling that the canon holds for so many people. In his interview, former principal dancer Donlin Foreman generously opened up about his inspirations, the ways that he interpreted and engaged with Graham's forms, and the long-lasting effect that the work has had on his life:

BWM *Do you find resonance with the idea that the technique holds and passes on information specific to the female form? It came from Graham's body primarily and she was a woman and therefore there may be some unique information that comes from that practice which male, female, and others may absorb?*

DF *I did not know anything of the technique when I joined the Company. I did not know anything of the repertoire when I joined the Company. It was like stepping into the deep end of the swimming pool and learning to swim. And so where it seemed everyone else did the technique and then the repertory, I was cross-referencing hysterically to be able to make it all work. I approached technique very differently. I never felt like demanding the counts, people were so precious about demanding that thing is on this count. What mattered to me was the vessel of the body and that people recognized the contraction as an embrace or as an enfolding where the body opened up inside and made a place for the world. That it was infinite, it was not finite.*

That the release was the letting go of everything we had let go in our lives, all of the people we had seen and said goodbye to. So in those two remarkable movements the world was held and everything else stood on top of that. It was always this image of me learning my prayers to be able to continue. The reality was that they divined angels' graces and that my feet were planted in the clay of the Earth and the oppositions within in me raged between those points. And so opposition was very real to me; it was not a word, it was not an action in the technique. It was all of living. The technique to me was a serious voice that rose up from inside and that was honed by those movements.

Foreman recalls here one of his teachers who was also one of Graham's most prolific dance partners, Bertram Ross:

And because he is not here, I like to say that I went over and subjected myself or submitted myself to Bertram Ross who was teaching these other classes outside of the studio because he had been excommunicated. I was sitting in the class one day, we were doing spirals around the back and he stopped in the middle of the fourth position spiral (and I had always loved these things). I never did the technique well, but I loved going through it. He stopped and he called out a woman on the right side of the classroom.

He said simply, "Stop, you can't do this that way, you have to love it to do it the way it should be done." Something in me absolutely opened up and I realized that that is what I did. I knew what he was saying. Not that I understood what he was saying, but I knew that love of the doing. I was always amazed that the word love was not used in the studio. Martha never said that, except one time she said, "Well maybe I did love Erick." I don't have any Martha stories about the technique. I feel like it was her challenge to discover. She would chide and say, "I resent having to tell you these things because I had to discover them myself."

I always felt that using the movement of the contraction, taking a contraction, the movement of pulling in was definitely a female gesture. But by working through it, I understood it as the opening of a vessel and embraced that. It doesn't work if we can't make things our own, so it became my own. It became my knowing of my own vessel. I felt that my role was to be a post in the middle of the stage, something anchoring the place that the woman moved around, and that in order to do that I had to pull the ground into myself. These are hindsight things; it was the action that was the moment, the doing. In hindsight afterwards, you can look back and say oh yeah that was that, but it was a very real feeling of pulling the ground into you.

I realized that I had three teachers who were equally influential with the technique and the repertoire. They were Martha Graham (the rep, the technique), Rilke[11] (his writings), and William Blake's watercolors and etchings. A book of Rilke and a book of the etchings were always with me, and I don't think that I would have known as much about fulfilling the technique or these movements if I had not realized the universality of them through Rilke's writings. The movements that Blake described visually in his technique or his way of showing movements of the body. I was very, very, very drawn to that and as a choreographer it influenced a lot of the movements that I was doing.

Foreman continues with an insight from a company tour to London:

On that tour in 1979 … we went into the Tate in London, and they had a whole section that was devoted to Blake's work and it was all laid out in these cabinets in a darkened room and there were tables that you looked into. I remember Jacque [Buglisi] and I walking through these rooms, and I remember he had laid out Martha's technique in the 1800s truly. There was a pleading, there was a high lift, but they were all contextualized, they were real. They were not the technique that we do in a void in the classroom to build physical prowess. They had clarity and context. I bought that book at that exhibit, and that was one of my bibles for forever. It is in pieces now on my shelf over my desk. To say the pelvis is the center of my existence is real.

---

[11] Poet Ranier Maria Rilke 1875–1926.

I don't know how I came to the Graham house. Truly I feel like I was fated to do that. When I started dancing, the road drew me directly there through Jacqulyn. I had no idea about it, and as I see it now, because I stepped out of the dancing community, it was to learn how to live. When I would teach, people didn't have much patience with me because it wasn't about the Graham technique—it was learning about our lives and our living. It all went back to two things. It comes back to the embrace and the letting go, and I don't hear anybody talking about that. And it's about this four-letter word "love" that has nothing to do with letters and everything to do with being able to hold in this vessel everything we think we can't. So everybody's take on the work is different, and that's mine.

This is the thing with the technique and all this. The life doesn't live in understanding; it just lives in uncovering our knowing. That was the aspect of the technique—of sitting on the floor, of subjecting yourself to sitting on the floor. I read a thing in a book called Parabola, *and it talked about the Oracle at Delphi being a three-legged cauldron with a top on it. And on the top sits the goddess through whom the oracle is uttered. And that her sitting on this place denotes possession, and when we walk in and we sit, we don't have to be subjected to the place, it becomes ours—we possess it. We don't have to pay money for it, we don't have to do anything except be there completely and do. It's infinite, all of the images are infinite.*[12]

Donlin Forman's use of imagery and overflowing passion for art are evident in his words. His use of poetic and classical art references also reveals the ways in which dancers develop their own interpretations of work and ultimately their own artistic voice. Allowing emotion to flow through metaphors and ultimately through dancing affirms our humanity. It is our emotion that allows us to feel compassion, build our strength, and embrace the whole of living through our dance. The wholeness of life is contained in dance when we allow our emotions to express in concert with our physicality. Even now, well into the first part of the twenty-first century, humans are searching for new ways of understanding our make-up, how we repress urges, and what that repression may unleash when left to fester. Ritual and repetition create energetic imprints into space with breath, shapes, and movement dynamics which can be freeing and healing.

Working in a very different voice and body from Graham, yet addressing similar themes in her work, poet Audre Lorde, whom I choose to reference here, speaks to erotic energy and oppression in her essay "The Uses of the Erotic: The Erotic as Power." She expresses an artist raging against dominant culture and activating her emotion, intellect, and understanding of physicality to express an alternative way of living. Lorde writes:

---

[12] Personal interview with Donlin Foreman.

Recognizing the power of the erotic within our lives can give us the energy to pursue genuine change within our world, rather than merely settling for a shift of characters in the same weary drama. For not only do we touch our most profoundly creative source, but we do that which is female and self-affirming in the face of a racist, patriarchal, and anti-erotic society.

When I speak of the erotic, then, I speak of it as an assertion of the life-force of women; of that creative energy empowered, the knowledge and use of which we are now reclaiming in our language, our history, our dancing, our loving, our work, our lives.[13]

In reading Lorde's writing, I experience both phenomenological and physical connection to the work that Graham did in creating the Martha Graham Dance Company. It is a vehicle to experience the erotic as "an assertion of the life-force of women; of that creative energy empowered." Graham and Lorde may not be a natural pairing for some, due mainly to generational differences and experiences of racial oppression and activism, which are huge themes of Lorde's work. Even so, I chose to bridge Graham with Lorde's life-affirming passages that speak to women (and all peoples) through generations who are empowering themselves through physicality, sexual liberation, and self-expression. Illuminating the female form through the effort and art of doing is the common ground. Movement has meaning, and movement creates meaning.

Teaching and Learning through the Feminine Lens

Teaching is a humbling experience that has located me in a place of abundance. I have come to see ways in which the daily dance practice opens and strengthens people of all ages to get in touch with the little dance inside and open up to hear their inner rhythm. A daily practice of listening and dancing teaches us about our own, personal next direction.

There is a profound satisfaction in witnessing young people become self-possessed inside of their changing bodies and discovering their bodies as a world. With permission I share an excerpt of a letter from one of my former students, Isabella Pagano. She attended the Fiorello H. LaGuardia High School for Music and Art and the Performing Arts, aka "the *Fame* school" in New York City when I was a teacher of Graham technique there. Her expression of self-awareness and curiosity move me to emotion each time I read her words:

I'm not sure quite how to word this, so sorry if this gets a little confusing. It has always been difficult to really appreciate or reveal my femininity.

---

[13] Audre Lorde, *The Uses of the Erotic. The Erotic as Power.*

FIGURE 12 Steps In The Street. *Senior dancers at LaGuardia High School in New York City perform in their graduation concert. Dancers: Angelina Hoffman, Isabella Burton, Emily Dean, Kyra Ferguson, Emily Young. Photo by Scott Allen.*

I'm generally more comfortable in masculine clothes and with my hair pulled back. I feel a freedom and strength in what my clothes give me, despite their being pretty un-feminine looking. So, for me femininity in dance was always closely tied with beauty and grace, but lacked empowerment and the strength I had felt in how I dressed. Your Graham class has showed me that femininity is strength. There is a beauty and power in just being a woman or a girl. But also that femininity doesn't need to be beautiful, it can be bare and guttural and exposed. Knowing this has allowed me to explore movement and myself in completely new ways. Since being in your class, I think I have much more embraced my femininity rather than trying the shove her down.[14]

In these few sentences Miss Pagano supports the idea that Graham created a body of work that empowers people. The work was not only about Graham herself, it was and it is about the experiential range human emotion. Theater is a state of awareness and action toward evolution of the self in

---

[14] Isabella Pagano, seventeen at the time of writing.

concert with others; it is the practice of accepting an existential challenge. In engaging the urges that motivated her, Graham lit the way for so many. She said: "The force of god that plunges through me is what I live for."[15] She shared her inner landscape—those images she returned to again and again, the well from which she drank, with us.

In the following interview we hear from Maria Gaviria Hurtado, a dancer/teacher/arts leader from Bogotá, Colombia. Gaviria Hurtado studied and taught Graham technique but did not dance the repertoire. Her poetic experiences with the technique, however, show the significance that its agency and philosophies bring into the life of any dancer who chooses to engage it.

LMGH   *When we danced, I don't remember if it was Bob or Nathan,*[16] *but they said women dance from the vagina and men pretend like you have one. And we had a lot of guys. Graham's technique comes from the vagina, from a sexual place, deep like a root. One of the pieces that I most loved in my life is a piece about how women breed their children for war and they lose their children (because that was happening here).*[17] *The men and boys go to war but the great loss, even though there is a lot of loss for everybody, is the women who keep breeding their children to send to war and to lose them to war. And so in this piece that we did with six men and six women, when we danced it was very emotional for all of us because* [the directors] *asked us to take from our personal stories of violence here in Colombia. We created all of this together. There is power in the way that a man will dance and explore and convey power, but I do believe that there are things that only a woman can do and transcend through her body because we are givers of life—that is just a fact.*

It is not about being objectified nor about feminism. But women bring to the table things that men cannot and men bring to the table things that women cannot. It does not mean that we are not equal, we are. We both have strengths which benefit both. I think that Graham is a technique that is best for a woman's body, but it is beautiful when a man can approach it and allow himself to be transformed through it because it gives him a deeper understanding of his own self. It is not about feminine or masculine, it is more about a place of compassion, a place of passion, of pain, of understanding your own internal connections and emotions. In my belief [men] *have been taught* [through patriarchy] *to cut emotion, men don't cry you know.* [Patriarchy dictates that] *men are caregivers and take care of women which are weak and less, and so men cannot express their feelings because they always have to keep a very big front. But I think in Graham men are allowed to explore that in a very deep way, which is*

---

[15] "Martha Graham: The Dancer Revealed," *American Masters*, 1994, season 1, episode 2.
[16] Professors of Dance at Southern Methodist University in Texas, USA.
[17] Referencing her native home of Colombia.

great, and it also puts them in a vulnerable position.

It is not stated, but when a man practices Graham he is more vulnerable than women. When a woman does Graham, it is easy for her to find empowerment through this movement and to follow something that is tribal; a man has a different process because he has to become vulnerable in order to feel, which is a process that is beautiful and inspiring through feeling his body as a woman in a way. Being compassionate enough to get into a woman's shoes and feeling how she might feel. How might having a vagina feel? Even just doing a contraction—when does a man do a contraction? It is not natural in their lives. It is completely different for them, which makes them more powerful, but I think their process is about vulnerability and being compassionate. Understanding more a feminine movement not as weak, but a feminine movement empowered.

BWM *What you bring up for me is the philosophy of the courage to be vulnerable.*

LMGH *Exactly. When a woman thinks that now she has the power, where before she was being taken care of and now I am powerful enough, that is even scary. You know the image of the Pieta, when you see the image of the Virgin which is carrying supposedly the savior of the world I mean, who holds the power. It is not about power, but it is about power. It is about how we complement each other—how we have to find the greatest power, and the greatest power is through unity and it is female and it is male. Be vulnerable but be strong.*

It goes into so much more than just dance class because you translate that into a violent place where we were, and I think that allowed me to work on my trauma. We had a really hard time when Escobar overtook the [Medellin], but I think that Graham allowed me that. I was privileged in many ways but I was very hurt in many others. I was trying to heal and my body has always been my vehicle to exorcise all of this. You are making me think of a lot of things today that are very beautiful and healing.

BWM *Art can heal or transform.*

LMGH *Yes! That is why I work where I work. Art is going to help you to travel through things. In 2000–2 I was able to teach Graham technique in the State College called ASAB—The Academy of Arts of Bogotá and I was like, "What am I going to teach these people?" In Colombia people come into college from all types of backgrounds, so I said, "What makes sense for me?" What was really natural and I knew really well was Graham technique. So, I had these kids five days a week for two and a half years, and my basis of what I gave them was Graham class every single day. It was beautiful because I could actually see how their bodies changed. It was natural; I was convinced that what I was teaching them was going* to benefit them in every single sense and that it was a good complement to folkloric. It was all coherent. I taught what I had been taught, and practiced it with them because I loved doing it. You know how you get into this zone and you do the bounces and you just go … up to this day I do my little class here on the floor as a way of being present with my center, with my whole body actually.

Graham really helped me. It was useful for a lot of things that were not necessarily class or repertory. I had one moment where Graham [technique] *saved my life*. This was [in] my first solo piece, which is still being performed today. It was a piece about the first man in my life. The stage was filled with drinking glasses and I would dance in between the glasses. I would break some, it was very controlled, but if I knocked down the wrong glass at the wrong moment I could be injured. At one moment about twenty minutes into the hour-long piece, I had to put the glasses one inside the other. That night it was the premier, and the director had told me that "if for any reason something happens and you break the glasses we will turn on the lights and ask the people for a moment and we will clear the stage for you." At twenty minutes into the dance with the column of glasses on top of me, the glass in the middle broke and they all fell to the floor. Twelve glasses broke all around me. I looked up and the lights continued, the music continued. I was there sitting with a full audience thinking, "What am I going to do?" The way that I got out of it was a Graham spiral—this is true. I was sitting in a fourth position on the ground so I just did a spiral and pushed my self up with the least amount of pressure on the floor because I was stepping on glass. I spiraled out of there taking the weight up and so I got out of that. I finished the piece inverted and got glass in my knees with two rivers of blood dripping from my legs. All of this was done in silence with the audience in front of me. This was the craziest thing. Everybody thought it was meant to be like that. It was the Graham spiral—it was the only way and it was automatic because it was in my body. That was one of the most incredible moments in my dance life.

BWM   *Thank goodness you had technique!*

LMGH   *Because I would always train and when I gave company class I would give Graham because it was my favorite. It was where I felt very strong. It is a movement for my body, mind, and soul. It is a universe that I love, it defines me, I consider myself a Graham dancer. It shaped my career and my life as a dancer. It helped me to get strength that is sometimes hard to find. You know as a dancer we are trying to be what is so unattainable but with Graham I felt, "I got it." It gave me a passionate peace.*

BWM   *With such a rich dance tradition as you have there in Colombia, how do you think that dancers in Colombia benefit from learning a technique of modern dance such as Graham?*

LMGH   *I think when you are serious about dance there are places of technique where, regardless of what you do, whether it is folklore or tango or ballet or salsa or any type of modern or contemporary dance, you need to be able to handle your center to begin. You need to be able to handle the space around you, have strength in your feet, to turn, it applies to every type of dance. Secondly, when you have technique you will be able to advance and be more versatile. Some people fall in love with salsa, tango, cumbia, others with burro, with ballet or contemporary, and you will find what fits your body and fits your spirit.*

But through all of that when you have technique, it is freeing. When we talk about technique, we usually go to ballet right? But when you talk about Graham, it is three-dimensional, involves the spiral and the contraction in a way that no other technique does. I mean you see it everywhere, and when you don't know that you are using it, you flail. Have you seen salsa? It's all there. In tango, it's all there. When you understand the concepts, you can apply them everywhere and then you see what you like. When you have a strong concept and a strong foundation, it shapes your body in a way that gives you freedom and versatility.

Indeed, the technique empowers women, men, and others to feel their strength through surrender and vulnerability formed from the place of authority and agency. Graham's practice of creating emotion-based movement from rigorous physicality and breath is her deepest and most far-reaching influence. The by-product of this was that people who practice it become physically aware of their own strength and ability to claim agency through their bodies. Graham's work has always stood in stark contrast to commodified dance for commercial gain in that she was not creating spectacle. Graham did not creating dance for entertainment. Her dance was about the body itself, discovery and art.

Intermission

I am tuning my instrument, my body. My teeth grit as I lay on the floor rolling out my muscles which have wound up tightly around the bone. No room, no freedom.
In this process, I look for the painful spots and go into them hoping for release.
Is this a metaphor? Growth does come through pain.
The dance is still teaching me—about life.

> Like the pull of a bow
>
>   across
>
>   the string
>   the landscape affects me.
>   I take in the tone of my experience,
>   then release its resonant song.

(Blakeley White-McGuire)[18]

We hear again from current company dancer Leslie Andrea Williams on the subject of personal agency:

LAW   *I really love that the work was created by a female. I think it is important to understand how the sexual center forms the work. People in the Company, when you get coaching, can be a little bit prudish about it or dance around the word, but there was one time in a rehearsal of* Diversion of Angels *when Janet[19] said, "This piece is about the vagina." We said, "OK, yes it is." And there are other times when coaches have said, "You really have to move from your sexual center" or "It's about the sensuality of the woman," etc. I mean, yes! Absolutely, that is what I love about it.*

BWM   *It should feel good!*

LAW   *It should feel good, and I think that it is interesting to think about these parallels of pleasure and pain. They are very connected, and I think that when it comes to being a female those aspects are what make up what it means to be a woman. Giving childbirth, having a child is a painful experience, but also extremely pleasurable to bring a new life into this world. The female body is beautiful, and the way it is accentuated and presented in Graham technique is beautiful and architectural and highlights the beauty of the body in a way that is different from, say, ballet.*

---

[18] Tour journal entry.
[19] Janet Eilber, Artistic Director of the MGDC.

BWM *Does the idea of feminism resonate with you in your Graham work at this point?*

LAW *I actually googled "archetypes of feminism," and the first thing that came up was this cheesy archetypes of seduction by a female. I will read some of them the siren, the sophisticate, the boss, the bohemian, the goddess, enigma, empress, ingenue. It gave descriptions of each one, and some of the archetypes are relating to the female in relationship to the man. And then some of them are standalone, but all of them, if I think about all of the roles I have seen that Graham has in the repertoire, I think she touches on all of those archetypes. Sometimes there are more than one archetype in one role.*

For me I would say that I am a feminist in the definition of equality for all genders. I don't know if Martha Graham necessarily felt that way about feminism. There are different aspects of feminism where the female is it. Like God created women and women rule the world. No. I think men play a part, and in her work there are definitely levels to what it means to be a female. I read a lot of Carl Jung, and I think that the female can be both masculine and feminine and the same for the male. My opinion is that all masculinity is toxic masculinity. I don't believe in patriarchy, and I feel that the world would benefit from a humanistic, it does not matter the gender, understanding of archetypes.

That there are feminine and masculine forms. Jung talks about animus and anima, that we all have both. I think that in society we feel like we have to hold one in a higher regard than the other, and it doesn't seem to work out very well. So I like that Graham understands that the female can be many things: she can be strong, she can be weak but she is still human and has a story to tell and a way of being that is not the traditional sense of what it means to be female. I am still understanding though what her relationship is to the man in her work. It seems very cut and dry like, "This is a man, a big strong man!" Maybe it was because of the time, she was getting people who were coming straight from the army to come and join and do these roles. She loved a big strong man to come and lift her up. I can appreciate that. I am still trying to understand what it is to be a man in her work. I am curious about that.

Graham's body of work has opened many people's minds to seeing dance as art, and through multiple lenses. Williams' curiosity about Graham's treatment of male roles or characters within her repertory demonstrates the breadth of terrain which we have yet to till. There is just so much fertile material to address through research and response.

Master teacher and muse Terese Capucilli shares her experience of the language of the work and various ways that innovation continues to emerge through it:

TC   *In terms of the Graham language, what we have learned and what has developed to be the Martha Graham technique has so many different forms through the generations of dancers who have lived through it. All of these different forms have developed within the generations that helped to mold the technique. So even though, well, we think about Martha and all of her women in the very beginning of time; in terms of Martha and her opus, the idea of it coming from the female body is so minute compared to what it has given and how generationally it has developed. Because it has not just been danced or learned by females. Even the work that was done very early on with the technique became easily part of the male form. So I do not think about it as male/female except within the context of how things developed within the work itself. But in terms of the language that we learn which to me is kind of a form of poetry of the body; it has gone through so many generations of dancers.*

Martha was very much a part of that process of how it developed, was very much of the moment to change things and develop things within the technique. [She would] take things from the work she was creating and bring them into the studio as part of her technique, which she never meant to make anyway. It became a language for us, it became a physical language—it became something that we wanted to inhabit. So I do not ever think about it as, well it emerged from the female form, and it stayed in this female form and it is only for the female form. It is more about how the technique morphed or changed or kind of fed through these different threads of not only the individuals that came through the studio. I am not just talking about those that actually were in the Company, but even students that came to the studio. What happens when those students leave, those different voices?

I think the technique allows for those different voices because it is such a codified language. We have the codified language. We know we are going to go from the bounces to the breathings to the threes and sixes, but how the voice of teacher comes out in that is varied. Many times I think about little houses of places that have come to teach the Graham technique ... and again I am talking about the technique. The language not Martha's repertoire, but how the language has moved. There are these little houses and places where students are learning not only the language but certain philosophies that come out of the delving in, and it really has to do with who is in front of the room. What their experiences are and what they find to be important in the technique, which is not to negate anyone. Because the feeding of that information historically to the body, which generates a great exploration of human beings at their core, is really more important than whether it is a female form or how it embraces the male form.

We can look at that differently when we are talking about the repertoire. If you are talking about repertoire you can kind of get this imbalance of the kinds of movements that the men do compared to the female movement, but ultimately we are all using the same language to get where we have to go. But you can also see the beautiful sensuality and expressiveness, let us say vulnerability, which is not something you always see on stage in a male form. Some of the work does show that, Hecuba's son in Cortege of Eagles *[for example].*

I think that there is a wonderful, and it would be interesting to see, the pathway that the technique has taken from not having a spiral and then the spiral started emerging as dancers progressed. As you know, when Martha was alive she was so living in the moment. The dancers also, through the generations got stronger, more versatile, and the technique became incredible and things started to emerge and to develop in a very different way. So I do not think you can pinpoint just one aspect of sexuality in that way, in gender.

… When I talk to my students, I talk about the place of life. The female of course has the receptacle of the life and can understand that inner feeling, but when do they feel that? I do not feel that the male cannot have that same sense. Yes, I am a female so I know what it feels like in my body, but certainly the sensuality and the way that we can delve into what I call "the place of life" and having that golden egg in the center of your pelvis and everything moves into that golden egg [can be felt by all sexes]. *Through the chakras of the body and up through, how we can bring that up through to the solar plexus and beyond. But I do not see and I do not teach to the female body the expressiveness that can be brought into the body through the technique.*

In the way that I see the generating of the initiating of Martha's work, we talk about the pelvis. The pelvic truth and generating the contractions and the releases from the pelvic floor. I do not see that any differently engaged than through a female or a male. I also see if from even a deeper place energetically, that it's actually from beyond the body, it's actually coming from below the feet that the contraction is coming. So it is generating certain kinds of energetic feeling through the body that can be taught whether it is a female body or it is a male body. That is just my opinion of it, and it feels different on every body and it will look different on every body. And some people will never understand it, those kinds of sensations, but sensations are also things that are incredibly important to the technique.

I do not think that you can teach the technique without understanding sensation and energy in the space. There are many different ways. In terms of tactile ways that I teach, touch is so important. As soon as you touch a student or you have them touch their own face or have them touch their own heart, the artist brings those sensations because of their memory. It also goes back to what you were saying about the female body too. You know Martha always talked about the body like a computer; it has an enormous memory bank. So what is that? I always talk about the center of the hand and how much history, the generations of people through the blood stream. So those kinds of things are really important in the teaching of the technique. To keep the expressiveness very human, very poetic—it is not self-indulgent (of course Martha hated self-indulgence), it is not that at all. It is ironic in a sense, and I have been thinking about this a lot through the years in the way that I have worked. The way that I have taught others to think and it has to do with the irony of—as an artist learning the technique, you have to go so far in that it feels like a very selfish place to be. However, when you have come to a place where you understand that passion and curiosity in the body and that generational pull you know, that memory bank that is inherent in every ounce of blood in your body; it actually becomes selfless. And those are the artists that I want to see on the stage. Those who have delved so deeply into what others might see as a very selfish way.

And that also really helped me in my own career to stay the course. Because role upon given role upon role of Martha's—to be able to stay at the caliber of integrity where you know (and you know) where you need to be. You know you need to stay there. What is keeping us there? How do we manage to be there? And for me I came to the realization that it was more than just me on the stage, and that is Martha's work. That is the beauty of learning it from the very base, from the very philosophy of it. Sitting on that floor in the studio, practicing day in day out that ritual. You know, how you stand up in the beginning of the class for your teacher—for your space [then] sit down on the floor. Once you understand that kind of ritual, that kind of practice, that kind of task putting that on yourself, then you can start the exploration inward—that can then give. So when I would be learning something new that would frighten me, I had to constantly tell myself, "it is not just you, you are every woman." And the same with any coaching I did. This is how I feel, particularly when working with students, how I got them to not be so fearful of where they were going but to keep the task. To know where you need to climb the mountain, be up there then drop down, maybe okay, then you just climb up again. That is the life. That is the life we lead, and I feel like a lot of the irony between the selfishness of an artist and the selflessness ultimately is where the freedom comes. It is complicated to understand, and it can go back to just Martha's whole concept of simplicity. And there is also the quote of Leonardo Di Vinci that says "simplicity is the ultimate sophistication."

Everything is so intertwined emotionally, physically, spiritually. I do feel that this house of pelvic truth in any body can be expressed. I think because I did all female roles, of course I am going to delve into those places, those memories of that character in a way that becomes an expression out of my own female form because I identify as a female.

As far as I am concerned, whether you are going to be a Graham dancer or not, this idea of the miracle of the human being really is so important. The kind of language that we use as Graham artists, there can be such a curiosity. As soon as I have students, the first thing that I talk about is the curiosity that is so beautiful in a child, the way that children learn. Because the technique is so difficult to learn, if you don't approach it like another language ... being able to say, "I love you" is not enough. [Here Terese voices different expressions of I love you with varying qualities.] To be able to bring the expression, so learning each word of the technique is critical and the pathways from one thing to the other and the beauty of the stillnesses and the "and" count is critical.

I think I have a quote that Martha said: "If you have no form, after a certain length of time you become inarticulate, your training only gives you freedom." I don't know if you know that quote? I always tell my students, "I am not making Graham dancers, I am making expressive artists. I am giving you the opportunity to challenge the expressiveness in your bodies, to embrace life's adventures and the memory in your blood stream." I learned about Martha when I went to Purchase 1974–8, that is where I learned Graham technique and went right into the Graham Company. But on every level as an artist, I have held on to her words.[20]

The Graham technique has gone through many cycles of evolution beginning in the late 1930s through up to the 1970s and 1980s. Marnie Thomas, a master teacher of Graham technique, writes about this in her unpublished essay:

> What makes Martha's genius particularly notable is the fact that she not only broke the rules of the conventional art scene that confronted her in the 1920s and 30s, she spent her many creative years building up a unique set of innovative principles for future generations to utilize and/ or to rebel against.
>
> Any dancer interested in carrying Graham Technique forward inherits this dual responsibility of maintaining what is constant and enduring in the form of expression, while bringing fresh inspiration into making the changes necessary to remain viable.[21]

This is an important passage for both dancers and teachers as Thomas addresses dogma which can be stifling to creative action. She shares that through confidence gained in practicing embodied knowledge, individuals may find an idea from which to revolt or deepen. Graham created a body of work that leads a dancer to their personal physical authority. It does not exist to please others. It is a path of self-discovery that can also be shared

---

[20] Personal interview with Terese Capucilli.
[21] Marnie Thomas from an unpublished essay on teaching Graham technique.

in community with others. These exercises, and Graham's canon in general, create a roadmap for discovering our sensual selves from the inside out. I can imagine Martha Graham sitting on the floor in her space of discovery curious about her body and seeking to understand what else is there to know. I imagine her grounding her body to the earth's energy through her verticality and moving it off-center.

4

Endurance/Re-Birth: Her Dancers Take the Lead—Inspirations from Artistic Practitioners

It's about artists
in their own right shouldering the responsibility
to discover who a character is rather than
waiting to be told. Being part of the
process of discovery. She was a charioteer
who assembled the greatest array of the fastest
horses and dared to team them together
and drive them in one direction using no reins
only a voice and a vision.
Dancing has to be essential.

(Donlin Foreman)

There is no metaphor that encapsulates the life of a dancer—not a blooming flower or an ephemeral butterfly. We dance with destiny or, as Graham would say, inevitability by learning to silence the noise of the outer world and pay full attention to the revelations of the body.

In the 1930s and 1940s, modern dance was a politically charged act and dancers were its laborers and innovators. But if modern dance, the genre itself, was born from revolution and innovation, then what function does it serve to repeat history through repertoire? If a modern dancer is one who innovates through dance, then should we not continue to make new dances instead of repeating repertory? Can we attend to each of these simultaneously and keep equal vitality for both? Should that be a goal?

In this chapter, you will hear from the voices of the final generation of artists to dance under Graham and also from present-day company members. These artists take Graham's canon forward with their own visions of dance in the twenty-first century. Artistic Director Janet Eilber speaks to the future of the Martha Graham Dance Company, while Jacqulyn Buglisi and Richard Move share their work in differing yet connected ways. Buglisi reveals the miracle of the body and power in numbers through her performance ritual "Table of Silence," which uses archetypes and symbols to galvanize power and effect change. Move embraces Graham's rebellious, transgressive path as a performance artist to push past gender binary, revealing the essence of Graham's transgressive work which is freedom for the individual.

Two global projects, Movement Migration and Graham for Europe, are uniting Graham artists in diaspora around the world through performance, workshops, scholarly research, and, most importantly, community. In their interviews, we also experience inspirations from current members of the Martha Graham Dance Company and imagine future generations of dancers embracing and building upon its epistemology. At the time of this writing, the Graham Company continues on its path of innovation and inspiration in lineage as an international artistic force of nature.

> There has to be about you a transparency to receive the energy around you—maybe that's what genius is; I don't really know. Talent is the ability to experience life and to communicate the experience to others.
>
> (Martha Graham)

Under the current Artistic Director Janet Eilber, a star dancer and actress, the Company develops new repertoire from twenty-first century

FIGURE 13 Rite of Spring. *Dancers: Charlotte Landreau, Abdiel Jacobsen, Ben Schultz, Ari Mayzick, Lloyd Knight, Lloyd Mayor, Leon Cobb, and Alessio Crognale. Photograph by Christopher Jones.*

choreographers within the context of Graham's canon. Through her vision Eilber unpacks classical programming with pre-curtain introductions and innovative ideas to engage the public. In *Clytemnestra Remash Challenge* and *On the Couch*, she invited the public to re-envision Graham's dances through personal video projects. *Lamentation Variations*, Eilber's most notable visioning for the Graham canon, serves as an entry point for contemporary choreographers to create new dances in response to Graham's signature solo *Lamentation*. Eilber has continually developed innovative collaborations in both theater and digital formats. For example, in productions between the Company and Italian theater director Antonio Calenda, *Cercando Picasso* (a surrealist evening's muse on Picasso's life), and *Promoteo (Prometheus Bound)/Bacchanti (The Bacche)* for the Festival of Ancient Plays in Siracusa, Sicily, Eilber plucked sections from Graham's *Night Journey* and *Deep Song* as choreographic and imagistic devices for artistic collaboration.

In 2010, Google commissioned animator Ryan Woodward to create a Google Doodle honoring Martha Graham. "The Story Behind the Graham Google Doodle"[1] explains the significance of each of the gestures in the doodle. Google has continued to be a collaborator with the Graham Company by sponsoring residencies which bring dancers and digital artists together. In this interview with Janet Eilber, she talks about the progresses the Company has made in the twenty-first century and of her hopes for its future.

BWM *When did you become the Artistic Director of the Graham Company and how did that come about?*

JE *I left the Company to try other things movies, television, and Broadway, then marriage and children. I was involved in coming back to Graham during the court case. After the first decision came down, where it was decided that the Graham Center owned all of the archives, the costumes, the films, the videos all of our ephemera, I was brought in to head up what we decided to call Martha Graham Resources. I was asked find a way to organize all of that "stuff." I started working on the reconstruction toolkits, and we started applying for grants to save the videos and the films and create databases of the materials. In the course of those two or three years, the court case[2] continued, and in 2005 the Board*

---

[1] Google Doodle, https://www.google.com/doodles/martha-grahams-117th-birthday.

[2] During the early 2000s, years after Graham's death, the natural course of reconfiguring the Company led to inevitable transformation for the Martha Graham Dance Company. In a 2002 lawsuit, copyright of her dances was awarded in the main (with exceptions of *Seraphic Dialogue* and those dances already in the public domain) to the Martha Graham Center of Contemporary Dance. In her judgment, Judge Miriam Cederbaum decided overwhelmingly in the favor of the Martha Graham Center. On May 9, 2002 the metaphorical eve of that pivotal decision, the international dance community showed its support for the Graham Company through petitions and boycotts and an evening of dance billed as "Indisputably Graham." It was to be a re-birth of the Company under the direction of her star dancers, Terese Capucilli and Christine Dakin, that launched the Martha Graham Dance Company into the new millennium.

*invited me to come in as Artistic Director of the whole organization—
the School, Martha Graham Resources, and the Company. We had won
the court case for the most part, but we were $6 million in debt. In a
way it was a good thing to be so at the brink of destruction—it gave me
permission to try new things. We had to find a new way of doing things.
So LaRue and I set about questioning everything. And because I had been
in films and television and lived in Los Angeles for twenty years, I had an
outside perspective on Martha Graham. From all of those years, I realized
that 99.9 percent of the world had no idea who Martha Graham was.*

*So it aligned with my deeply physical and mental connection to the
legacy to find ways to share that extreme genius and the value of her
timeless expression. I felt that my life kind of lined up. I had the experience
needed to follow a path that opened the doors and invited people in—that
let people in on the big secret.*

BWM   *Going back in time a little bit ... would you talk a little bit about
the atmosphere of the Company when you were dancing and Graham was
still creating?*

JE   *I was in Martha's ninth life, if she was a cat. She had such a long
creative life that she had different periods, different phases. My phase was
the 1970s. She had recovered from a debilitating loss, which was not being
on the stage any longer. That was why they expected her to die. She was
quite ill. She was giving up alcohol as well. When she came back in the 70s,
she was celebrated—embraced by the new celebrity culture that emerged at
that time.*

*That was when People Magazine started and celebrities started being
on the cover of the National Enquirer in grocery stores. There was
just a new culture around celebrity. She was embraced by a variety of
people. Great twentieth-century artists: Truman Capote, Andy Warhol,
Jacqueline Onassis would come to rehearsal. Betty Ford would come to
rehearsal. Halston, of course, befriended Martha Graham and became
a big supporter. Nureyev and Fonteyn worked with us; Elsa Peretti,
Sandy Calder (Alexander Calder, she called him "Sandy"), and of course
Noguchi.*

*It kind of all came together in the 1970s so that she had a new role,
a new stage, and was celebrated as The Genius. That set her on a new
path of truly appreciating her own legacy. I mean, she had to appreciate
her legacy in order to claim the celebrity that was built upon it. So when
people say that Martha said, "Oh I want it all burned, I do not care what
happens after I am gone," that was just theatricality—her actions spoke
louder than words. She was totally involved in securing and perpetuating
her legacy through the bodies of the next generations of dancers, the
filming that we did, the reconstruction of her works—everything. That was*

my era, the 1970s, and she was very much with it, choreographing every day, touring with us. The Company was a mix of great characters like it always is. Working with all of those people, I made lifelong friends. We lost too many of them to AIDS, but like any generation of the Graham Company, it is a crazy family that is bound together by a belief in the art form, being onstage together, being on the road together. All of the elements are there that bring you closer because you rely on these people whether they are lifting you up in the air or helping with a costume change, or giving you Advil when you are out. They become essential to your life at that time. It is almost like being in the army. From what I have heard about being in the army—you trust and rely on these people and that was certainly true in my generation.

BWM   *The human losses during the AIDS epidemic were catastrophic to the dance community. In terms of the legacy, so many male dancers who were significant to Graham's creative work were lost. Men who embodied the work in a very sensual, particular way at that time. In addition to the individuals themselves, what do feel was lost from the Graham legacy?*

JE   *I think a major thing that was lost is the continuity of coaching and mentoring. We lost the way each generation (that is only about ten years apart in the dance world) would come into the studio to coach roles that they had performed or dances which were created on them—roles that must be passed on to the next generation. One of the things that I noticed after being away from the Graham Company for a couple of decades was to come back and realize that there just was not the same resources of men to call upon to come in and coach—to carry on that part of the legacy. The other thing that I think happened, but have not really thought about it being because of AIDS, in the 1980s and 1990s there was a great emphasis in the Company on the classics that were created for all women—the works of the 1930s. That emphasis did not allow the men in the Company to have the same experience as the women. Again, that speaks to continuity and the talent that you attract. Perhaps twenty years ago men were not so attracted to dancing with the Graham Company because their roles just were not as fulfilling as the women at the time. They were not onstage as much as the women. I do not know that that was directly influenced by AIDS, but it compounded the through line for the men in our company.*

The body politic is a seminal topic for discussion in the Graham canon. Many practitioners do not feel it necessary to ascribe significance to gender-based physicality and I agree with that in the main. However, it is undeniable that Graham was a female, identified as female, and that her body of work came out of a female body and experience of living.

BWM   *Is there any significance to the physiology of a technique coming out of a female form as opposed to a technique being directed upon a female form?*

JE   *First off, do not let me forget to talk about genitals because Martha stopped saying "dance from your vagina" and started saying "dance from your genitals."*
    Here are my thoughts. The technique was created on a woman's body, there is no way around that. It was created in a time when women's sensuality, especially when talking about a woman's vagina, was radical. Martha was attracted to the radical. She was also creating a language that was primal. Sex is primal. She was not thinking, "Gee, am I creating a dance language that is available to all genders?" It was coming out of her guts—literally. And it was provocative because it was primal—not escapist swans, flowers, and exotica. She was stripping things down to that elemental, human thing. You cannot talk about it without talking about sex. It is the most elemental creative act. Because her company was all women for the first ten years, I think the technique became very attached to a woman's body. I think because a woman's hips are generally more open because they are designed for childbirth, a lot of the exercises are easier for female. But at some point, Martha switched over to saying "dance from your genitals" rather than "dance from your vagina." The male genitals are in the same place as women's—at the base of the pelvis. That driving force through the pelvis generates through a man's skeleton the same way it generates through a female skeleton. I think it is a language that any gender can speak if they are speaking it correctly. If they really are using the root of the pelvis, the genitals motivate all movement. I think that for all genders, the thrust is involved so the journey is very similar.

BWM   *I want to remind you from earlier to not forget to talk about the genitals. Did you talk enough about the genitals?*

JE   *I did. Martha switched at some point. You know Bob Cohan told me a story about when he was first in the Company. One of the dances he went into was in the chorus in* Letter to the World. *Martha hired him after he had only studied for a few months and they went on tour to the South. Jean Erdman had not been cast as The Speaker yet. Martha was experimenting with different actresses, and he said that the woman doing the speaking was named Angela. One night right before the curtain went up Martha went over to Angela and said, "Tonight I want you to speak the lines from your vagina." And Bob said that Angela came up to him afterwards and said, "It was all I could think about for the entire dance— am I speaking from my vagina?"*

BWM   *She was not sure?*

JE   *And that is why I say that Martha was provocative. She knew that was provocative. It was essential to her creation, her art form, the revolution that she was launching. So that is what I wanted to say about genitals.*

BWM   *Do you think that this is where the moniker "House of Pelvic Truth" comes from?*

JE   *Totally.*

BWM   *Do you know the genesis of "The House or Temple of Pelvic Truth?"*

JE   *It is in* Blood Memory. *She talks about how amused she is that "my school has been called the house of pelvic truth," and then she tells the story about one of her dancers setting a dance at Juilliard. The punch line is that the Martha Graham Dance Company is the only dance company in the world where the men have vagina envy.*

While Eilber is known for her easygoing attitude and graciousness, she also has a fierceness about her. She cares deeply for Graham's body of work. Eilber has generated many new projects during her tenure; *Lamentation Variations* has been one of the most successful.

BWM   *What was the genesis for the* Lamentation Variations *as a component of opening the doors to the Martha Graham Dance Company?*

JE   *The idea that nobody knew who Martha Graham was combined with $6 million in debt forced us to become very creative with programming. And those two desires—getting out of debt and engaging audiences in a new way—aligned for me. Some of the first things I did was to add a spoken introduction to a program or add a spoken narration throughout a program—using media to fill the stage and also to give context to the audience. We were not just turning off the lights, doing a difficult dance from 1947, turning them back on and expecting everybody to know what the heck was going on. We were opening the doors, letting people in, and, like a museum audio tour, giving people context and things to look for.*
   In 2007, our opening night at the Joyce Theater happened to fall on the anniversary of 9/11, and in order to commemorate that date, we came up with a creative structure that was meant to be fast and provocative— and inexpensive because we did not have any money. We had tried all of these experimental things, so all of the groundwork was there. We asked three choreographers to do a one-night-only event—to spew out their choreographic responses to a film of Martha Graham dancing Lamentation. *We told them they would each get the same amount of*

money (I think it was $1,500), they would each get ten hours of rehearsal, and had to use public domain music or silence, simple costumes, no props no sets, and they had to keep it under four minutes because that is how long Lamentation *is.*

This was a project that could be done in several days, and Larry Keigwin, Richard Move, and Azure Barton agreed to do it. Each one of them broke a rule, but that was okay. On that September 11th, we showed the film of Martha dancing Lamentation *followed by those three dances— no pause, no stopping for bows in between. They were presented as a unit, and it was very powerful and effective.*

BWM   *How do you as Artistic Director bring in inspiration? What are your inspirations?*

JE   *Oh, what everybody else is doing and of course the Graham legacy. Every time I watch one of Martha's dances, whether it is in a film or rehearsal, I'll notice something for the first time, and I see how we can use that—how we can connect that in a program with this other thing? So I am always looking for strange connections. As these revelations happen to me, I try to remember them and think, Well, how can I provide that discovery to someone else?" And then I do a lot of looking at other people's work and to other art forms' successes that might work for us. It is challenging, but it is invigorating because we have really laid the groundwork for the idea that the Graham Company can do anything. It has taken fifteen years, maybe twelve years to build that reputation. We have done so many crazy and diverse things—from the Clytemnestra Re-Mash to our two-week residency at Google (experimenting with cutting-edge technologies) to our world-class performances at the Paris Opera House. We now are getting a reputation for running the gamut. The new reputation and growing audience interest means you can be kind of fearless, and say yes let's try it, let's do it!*

BWM   *When you receive a revelation about a piece, and then you think, "How can I give that experience to the audience?," that is profound.*

JE   *Well, it is the same thing you do, Blakeley. You as a wonderful interpreter of Graham and others who interpret Graham as well—you discover things about the character that you are beginning to inhabit, and you want to share them. You go, "Oh, that is what Jocasta is doing over there next to that bed. How can I let the audience in on that?" Because it is funny, you see, when you have those intimate revelations on a Noguchi set, it is not always easy to figure out a way to share it with 2,500 people out in the audience without mugging or using semaphore flags. That is the challenge of interpretation and in a way, my job is interpretation also.*

BWM   *Thank you. Is there anything that you feel is a misconception about the Graham Company that needs to be corrected?*

JE   *Oh yeah. We have been trying to overcome our reputation for being old and dusty and conservative. That was my first job when I became Artistic Director. And there are still a few people that cling to that idea. But as I said, more and more people are saying, "Woah, Graham is doing that?" So we like to keep surprising people. That has been my whole North Star for this journey as Artistic Director, is to shake people up and get them to rediscover the Graham Company and Martha Graham herself.*

BWM   *Looking at the significance of lineage, of person-to-person transmission. Are we at a place where that is still necessary, or is there enough ephemera around the canon that it is not so necessary?*

JE   *The Company is old enough now that we are seeing the pluses and the minuses. It is going to be up to whoever is directing the Company fifty years from now to see our legacy in context of their times. In the 1980s Martha Graham refreshed her ballets, changed the costume designs, etc., and there was a noticeable heightening of the drama in the performances. But in the last fifteen years the world has changed. People's impressions of Martha Graham have changed. There is a greater appreciation of her modernism. We have actually had to strip away what you might call lineage.*

Things—the techniques she used in the 1980s to keep her works refreshed and potent—really belong in the 80s. Now that we are in a new era, people are re-discovering the genius of American art of the mid-twentieth century. We are actually using our ephemera and alums who are still with us who can comment on it, to strip the dances back to Martha's original intentions. Now, that is much easier said than done because today's dancers do not dance like dancers did in the 1930s and 1940s. Martha loved that. She loved the new facility of each generation of dancer. She knew that audiences expected it, and she incorporated it into her dances. So we have to keep that balance of being twenty-first-century art with twenty-first-century dancer-athletes, but we also have to look at the decisions that she and Copland and Noguchi or Hindemith or Barber made as they designed the world for any given ballet.

What we can capture, maybe, is what Martha intended—the message she wanted to deliver—and hope that directors fifty years from now can figure out how to deliver that message in a way that the audiences of their era will recognize.

Another jumping-off point for development within the canon are Graham's documented and embedded philosophies.

BWM   *This leads to another aspect of Graham as philosopher. Are there any philosophies that shine for you?*

JE   *Absolutely! It goes back to talking about the root of the pelvis, the genitals. The empowerment of the individual—and that impersonalizes it too much. The essential philosophy for me is about your own self-awareness, and your own power, and how to get out of your own way to use it most powerfully. How to understand yourself and deeply assess what you can offer. That is at the root of every Graham ballet. It is at the root of her technique. It is her essential philosophy. That is why that letter to Agnes DeMille[3] is so popular. As people discover it, you and I think, "Oh god, haven't you seen that letter before?," but they post it on Instagram like it is coming to them, from the mount. It was Martha's belief that you do whatever you have to do to be who you are and give that impactfully to the world.*

BWM   *Would you speak about the Company today—the look of the Company, its spirit, your intention as the creative force behind the Company today and where you see it going?*

JE   *Yes, you know the Company today has a great sense of ensemble. I think it is because of the commissioning of new works. Different dancers throughout the Company are chosen to excel in different ways. Where in the past we were only dancing Graham works, usually the greatest roles were given to the most experienced dancers. And they still are in the Graham works, but a new choreographer comes in, and they may choose the youngest apprentice to star in his or her dance, and suddenly these new dancers are carrying the weight of a twenty- to twenty-five-minute dance on the stage, and in the next one they are in the chorus. The new choreographer may choose the most experienced dancers to be understudies. It has really skewed the former hierarchy and allowed the different types of talents in the Company to shine. That has equalized them in a lot of ways. In today's company, they are such a family, they are so supportive of each other, they are so tight. It is remarkable that shift from hierarchy to a community.*

I did not aim for it, I was just aiming for opening more doors to Martha Graham by commissioning new work, and that meant that we had to start auditioning in a different way. We auditioned not only for great Graham talent. but we would ask to see some phrases from our contemporary work and we could see people in auditions shine in a different way too. It has really shifted the artistry of the Company individually and as a group.

The future is not as easy to divine as it has been in the past. And it was always pretty difficult to divine in the Graham world. I think we as artists

---

[3] Agnes De Mille, *Martha: the life and work of Martha Graham.*

FIGURE 14 Primitive Mysteries. *Dancers: Christine Dakin and the Martha Graham Dance Company. Photograph by Nan Melville.*

know that we are one of the things that holds people together, and we just have look forward and continue to address the crisis in the country by offering points of access, connection, and, hopefully, revelations through art.[4]

Innovation has been a hallmark of the Graham Company since its inception. Here, in her interview, former co-Artistic Director and principal dancer Christine Dakin speaks about her work in the Graham canon, crossing cultural boundaries through her artistic perspective, her teaching practice, and innovating with her online dictionary of dance, database Terpsikon.[5]

Dakin shares the roots of her work within the canon:

CD   *It was really a love affair of the physicality and the theatricality and the literacy. Martha's intellect and her autodidact—the breadth of her reading and the breadth of her thinking that really drew me. That combination of physicality and intellect was always what struck me as the most rewarding and the most challenging and the most powerful. Working with her and working with the Company was everything that I had hoped that it would be. Seeing the work from the inside, performing it from the*

---

[4] Personal interview with Janet Eilber.
[5] Terpsikon, https://terpsikon.com.

*inside, working with Martha day after day, year after year, decade after
decade (well not quite decade after decade), decade after half a decade—I
got to connect all of those elements that drew me to the technique. The
physicality and the tremendous creativity of her as a woman and how she
situated herself in the world and how she worked.*

*For me those three things—Martha as a creative artist, Martha's
choreography, and Martha's technique—were always one thing. That
was my experience of how she was and how she worked. It seems to me
that that's been a very increasingly rare experience to be able to spend
that amount of time working that deeply in all levels of the work. That, I
think, gives a different kind of perspective on both the art itself and on the
technique—I suppose on Martha as well.*

*All of that experience sheds light on all of those things. So whatever the
differences are in the society or the way we think about dance or the way
people experience dance now, I venture to think that those fundamentals
of human nature and human experience in dance, there's a core about
that that remains the same. How you pass it on to generations who do not
share much in common with what you know is very difficult.*

BWM   Do you experience that now with the post-millennium generation?

*CD   Oh yeah. Absolutely. The goals all seem different. That quantity
rather than depth, or familiarity with many, many, many things rather
than the deep knowledge of something seems to be more common now.
And in many ways that is fantastic because we love to have dancers have
broad experiences of different kinds of ways of moving, different kinds of
ways of studying, of putting themselves onstage—just the richness of all
the things that are available, it's fantastic. But like kids in a candy shop,
sometimes it's just too much stuff and we end up with not enough time
to actually really get deeply into any one thing, for most people. There
are always some people who are able to really do that. But I think a large
number of people nowadays are forced to and are happy to experience so
many different kinds of things. And then I think finding how to get deeply
connected to that—to any one thing enough to go deeply anywhere either
themselves or physically—becomes more difficult. That's what I see as the
challenge of both the performer, the choreographer, and the teacher. It is
how you give people a way into that with the scattershot approach that
sometimes exists.*

*BWM   Is there a particular literacy that goes along with it—some desire
for an elevated sense of art or expression or cultivation of the being that is
not necessarily for everyone?*

*CD   I do not think that any more or less true of Martha than any other
great artist. Great art is very demanding. But to my way of thinking, the*

reason it becomes great is not because it designates itself as great. It is great because many, many people over a long period of time continue to think that it is great. In the same way that a cliché has a foundation in reality, the reason that people call it great art is because it's great art. The elements of the great art are many in any art form, and I think that it is perfectly true that many people are not interested in cultivating the being. They just want to dance. There are many people who love the theatricality of the work and there are many people who like a … It depends on what part of the Graham work you are talking about. Like any dance form, some people are gonna like it, some people are not going to like it. They might recognize it as being a great work of art, but they do not like it. Like I said, that is not something that is unique to Martha's work.

When you are talking about something that is so utterly connected with her choreography, which is the technique—if you identify the technique as part of the choreography, then that puts the technique in that same basket. And it is easy to say, well, "I do not like that." That I think is a mistake. That, I do not think is a useful way to couch the discussion of whether Martha's work is for everybody or not. I think that the way she discovered her body, the way she developed what became the technique is profoundly human, profoundly organic, and I think the core, the heart of that work, should appeal to practically anybody. I do not think there is a question of taste involved in being able to experience the technique, to use it to build a body, a soul, a person. I think there ought to be, and there are, probably many ways to present Martha's technique in a way that it is useful and appealing to practically anybody who is trying to work in dance. The trick is how to do that—not all ways are equally effective. You have to focus them differently for different audiences. What is the goal we are trying to achieve? But I think that lumping the technique into the choreography is not useful. In the same way that you would not look at a painting and say, "Well I do not like their brush strokes"; no, you look at a painting, and the painting is what the painting is. If you want to talk about the technique and how it is actually done and structured and all of that information about the technique that was involved to create it, that is separate. I think, unfortunately, dance suffers from having the technique lumped in with the artistic creation.

BWM   *A technique, a body of work that was built, not solely but primarily on a woman's body. Do you see a particular potential in this canon to be a catalyst for young women?*

CD   *I resist that whole conversation about built on a woman's body. A female technique, a female point of view—even as I, myself experienced it as being empowering to know about her as a woman and to approach her*

*work at a time when being an artist, except in dance, was mainly, probably
a male purview. And certainly what Martha had to experience when she
was growing up and growing up within the art form and doing her main
work in the 1940s and 1950s, what she had to endure and to work with—
it is inspiring. But that is on a personal level. I never had the experience
of Martha or her work as being female and more than male. That forces
you to define those two things, which is binary. I think that Martha would
be interested in moving away from that. So I think we end up talking
about stereotypes when we approach it that way. I do not know what
that is. I think that as a human being, it was inspirational to see Martha
maintain and continue to create despite the fact that she was a woman
and what she created was a body of work that was extraordinary and
from a female point of view because she was a female. And sometimes that
was overt, and sometimes that was not necessarily an overt choice on her
part. That was what she did. She was a woman, and she did it, therefore
it was for a woman. I do not know as I can say, in all of the repertory
and all of the roles that I have done, that her interest in what I think of
as male and female … she was more interested in the female perspective
because it was her and because I think a combination of her personal
experience and the society that she was growing up in, she found women
to be more interesting. I think she found women to be more powerful.
The relationship between male and female interested her tremendously,
both between people (male and female) and qualities (supposedly male
and female). I think that conflict, that interchange, that little rubbing point
where they meet was fascinating to her, not always pleasant particularly
but fascinating to her. It may be that women are more interested in that
than men, I am not sure. But I think it simplifies Martha and her work to
narrow it to a female perspective without defining more carefully what you
are actually talking about.*

*Certainly her works were female centered. The female, Martha, was
on the center of the stage she was the star; she was the main character.
There is no denying that. Whether she did that purposefully because she
was trying to empower women, I am not sure. I do not think so. She was
an artist, she was who she was; she created art, she was a woman, and it
skewed in that direction. But when we start talking about it theoretically
and then ascribe motive to her because of that, I do not know how useful
that is.*

*For me, with a certain amount of perspective, a certain amount of
horizon over there—always the experience of the technique, the experience
of the teachers who were my teachers, the dancers I saw, the dances that I
performed with, being a part of the creative process with Martha—every
single element of that experience was transformative. It was all the way
in, the way forward, the way to examine, the way to experience, the way
to reflect. Again, I am not sure that that is unique to either Martha's work*

or to me as an experience of Martha's work. But for me, what she created, what she gave, the way she created and gave all of that was a continuing lesson. It was a learning; it was an exploration. I do not see that as generosity. I do not think Martha was generous in that way; Martha did what she needed to do. And if you were a part of that, you were expected to and could enjoy and benefit from. You were expected to make use of all of that information and make a contribution to the art form. So not so much generosity, as that is the way it worked.

BWM   Could you describe some of the ways in which she created, perhaps one of your experiences of creative with her?

CD   Whenever I did a role for the first time, it was always like a gift appearing surprisingly on my plate in the morning. And approaching any of the roles that I did—talking to Martha or asking her, getting up the nerve to talk to her, hoping that she would share some thoughts about the work—always very much included what she read. I think that she early on understood that I was a voracious reader of the literature of theater, the literature of the philosophy of theater. All of the other art forms that go into that were inspirations for Martha and were familiar and interesting to me. So it was always very precious to hear her talk about what she was reading what she was thinking about. She expected you to do what you did. And things that were interesting to me were maybe not interesting to other dancers. So with other dancers she shared other kinds of things. She was not particularly forthcoming about how to dance the dances. She was very much of the school of thought of, "I figured it out, you go figure it out," which is brilliant. Because then you do, and she tells you if you have gotten it or you did not. And then you go back and do it some more until she thought that you actually had achieved something with that. Trying to apply Martha's reading, Martha's understanding of human nature, trying to figure out Martha as a person always gave back a tremendous amount information that had to do with performing the works and being a person. So the task of trying to figure out what she wanted, trying to figure out how she arrived at the place to create something. And after many, many years you walk into the studio with her, and you begin to have a sense about what she was interested in—what her mood was, what she was struggling with at that point both psychologically and choreographically. So you just blundered around with your best guesses as to what might provoke something for her, inspire something, or irritate her—something. So there was never really a model, and each work that she did was a different world.

   When we did, for example, Phaedra's Dream, which involved Nureyev and involved a lot of hands-on work when Martha was older, it was really fascinating to watch her, to see her revert to a young girl in relationship to the man and acting out and experiencing all three of the characters. It was very vivid how she was picturing what was going on. Tapping into her experience while she while she was doing it, being it in the studio with us was fascinating.

BWM   Was that something different from acting, more accessing something in the moment of her personal experience?

CD   I think both. Martha was nothing if not a complete actress. But any great actress only gets there by having something deeply inside that they have figured out how to access. So it was a combination of those things. And it was not all sweetness and light. There was not a question of everybody was happy and we all had a good time, it was all rewarding. No, it was a lot of very, very, very difficult, very unpleasant stuff in the creation of art and working with great artists. But even that stuff in the depth and with the clarity and intelligence of Martha—even the crap was a tremendous source of learning and experiencing that one takes advantage of.

BWM   Does the phrase the House of the Pelvic Truth have any connotation to you?

CD   When you are in the kind of completely circumscribed, unique, of necessity self-protective world, you develop language and stories and games that you share. It is a society, it is an anthropological thing that happens. So a lot of the things that you hear that sound funny, are funny, they are usually said with a smile but they come from very true observations or experiences. So those kinds of things, the House of the Pelvic Truth or the Temple of the Pelvic Truth, all of that kind of stuff, either or both came from a dancer, ourselves, and of Martha. Or came from somebody making fun of Martha, and we adopted it and took on for ourselves. I never heard Martha say anything like that.

BWM   How about "the center of the stage is wherever I am"?

CD   Martha was a very funny lady. She was a great humorist, and I can easily imagine or hear her saying that as kind of a throw-away line, a joke, that now becomes this philosophical statement of something depending on who you ask.

BWM   It circles back to making a caricature of her makes her safer to deal with for some people, and I am trying to get past that. People say Graham was egotistical or a diva—I am trying to illuminate the humanist whom we follow literally in her footsteps. Because she was a great teacher in the mystical sense.

CD   *It is a worthy goal to try and combat that. She was as guilty as anybody of engendering that, at the same time, it is such a simplistic, unidimensional way of looking at somebody. I have to say I find it sexist, ignorant; I find it offensive. I do not think many people would use those kinds of words in describing a great male artist, all of whom were every bit as egotistical and egocentric and theatrical as Martha was. I find that a really good example of all kinds of generality and cliché and sexism, and sometimes coming from places that ought to know better.*

I think to credit Martha with the greatness of the art that she created— the establishment of the technique, the body of work, the maintaining of a company—I think one really has to remember how great that was. How incredibly difficult that was, what it cost her to do that. And not allow ourselves, or not be a part of diminishing her to one, seemingly egocentric, trait. When she was talking about being the center … You are talking about philosophically, spiritually, mythologically. There are lots of different circumstances, which, graphic artists and painters as well—there is a point which is the center. This is a purely practical artistic concept. Anybody who does not know that is perfectly welcome to think of it as, "I am the center of the stage and I am important," but for anybody who knows anything about art, it is making a corollary between other art forms and her art form. It is also deeply thoughtful and revelatory about the nature of being a performing artist. So no matter on what level you care to examine that statement, it does not bear egotistical as a description.

BWM   *I am coming from a place of wanting to articulate that the Martha Graham Dance Company, technique, canon—these were created by dancers, continued by dancers, and will continue based on the affection and will of dancers. Would you speak a little bit about "the lawsuit," when the dancers decided to close the Company and why?*

CD   *The way you cast the question is … the dancers did not close the Company. The lawsuit that was … decision was that if the Company itself was not allowed to perform Martha's works, then the dancers, those of us who were in the Company at the time, did not see how that could be. If we as a group of dancers were not to be allowed to perform her works, then in essence there was not a company. The decision was made that until … it was a boycott was what we did. Until the Company had acquired the rights to perform the work, the work would not be sold out in the world. There were lots of presenters and people who were concerned about that because they were perfectly happy to hire anybody to do a work without there actually being a company, but the dancers at the time decided that it was worth nearly anything to retain the rights of the Company as a unit to perform Martha's repertory. So the decision was made to go to court, to fight, and fortunately for the largest part we were successful in getting the rights to do that. It exactly asks the question, who has the right? In the end, the board of directors has the right. The dancers do not have the right.*

The dancers stuck their necks out. The dancers took the chances, and there were many, many people of all kinds, including the pro bono lawyers who helped us who through that—this was incredibly important. The last generation of dancers trained by Martha with the knowledge of the repertory, with the tremendous institutional knowledge, should be the ones who have the rights to perform the work. And the boycott itself was extremely successful. It was international, with thousands and thousands of artists of all ages and levels and degrees of well-known-ness who were appalled by what was happening and very supportive. Many people took it as a warning. I had Paul Taylor thank me. Yes, he thanked me, he said, "I'm sorry it happened but thank you. Now we know what we need to watch out for." There were lots of people who felt that way, because up until then, there had been instances of artists not taking the kinds of precautions that are now seemingly so obvious for the maintaining the rights to their work. And this was really a wake-up call for a lot of people. It is not simple, it is not straightforward, it does not necessarily go the way you want it to go. So I think that was kind of a seismic shift in the way artists started thinking about how to protect their work, themselves, their companies. It also, it brings up the larger question of who owns the work, and nobody has answered that question. Everyone comes up with a different answer. There are lots of different answers. But how do you own a work of art that is not an object?

BWM   *Would you talk about the work that you are doing now as an artist, the kind of dancing that you are interested in currently?*

CD   *It does all seem to stay connected. I have not escaped the curse of the Temple of the Pelvic Truth.*

BWM   *Why can't we escape it, and why do we want to escape?*

CD   *Anything that is that grand, that important, that powerful is certainly open to all kinds of abuse, and Martha had a lot of abuse heaped upon her. A lot of it is self-inflicted. Having expectations and doing things the way you need to do and want to do—it rubbed people the wrong way. And there is a lot of jealousy; there is a lot of stuff surrounding anything that is that successful and great. You cannot escape it. The knee-jerk negative clichés that are assigned and the reputation—the damaging of the reputation of both the technique and maybe the art is tragic, and a lot of it is … when people whose life and function is to create art, to make art, to learn how to make art, and that is your function, that is your task, joy, your way in the world. That is not something that most people understand. People do not know what that is; they cannot imagine what that is. It is very easy to be dismissive or critical of that, which does not absolve us from the kinds of negative, selfish behavior that make people very unhappy and angry with what they see as selfish bad behavior. People do not like to be abused. So if as a teacher or a choreographer or a director or a performer you are abusive, people do not like it. When Terese and I took over the direction of the Company and we started traveling again, there were a lot of places, mainly universities and such, the touring program spent a lot of time all over the United States. Every college up and down all the coasts, all through the center—many, many places. And there were many places who with great trepidation to have a Graham masterclass because they remembered having teachers who were harsh, difficult, demanding, and a way of the technique that was painful. So we came up against that.*

That is a certain way of working. It had its time and place. It was an internal thing. Once you are working with a group of artists, that is a world that can contain that kind of approach. When you disseminate it, it does not really apply. The goal changes, so everywhere we went after the performances and the classes people would come up to us and say, "Oh, this is fantastic, give us more of this, this is wonderful. We had no idea that Graham could be so wonderful and so powerful and so beautiful." So we felt like we were beginning to shift the goal so that we could carry forward the work in a different way. So it was focused on people who were not there to just perform the work in a professional, company situation.

Personally speaking, I can take all of the stuff I developed with Martha: the choreography, the teaching method, the working with actors at the Neighborhood Playhouse and actors in other places. Working in a lot of different companies, a lot of different countries for a long, long period of time. I can take all of that stuff and I can do what I want to do to fulfill myself as an artist. The subtext for me is how do I share this in a way that opens up the possibility that people will appreciate and understand Martha's work better—have a better, more complete experience of it that I can transfer some of the information that I have or some of the method that I have developed and received from my teachers in such a way that I can pass that on to non-dancers, to dancers, to audiences to other teachers. That is a twin, myself comes first: "How do I continue to develop and challenge myself and do new things, and how do I use what I am doing to give people more information about Graham the way I know it?" Those are two challenges because there is something profoundly unique about being an artist that is not easily communicated and certainly not easily understood. Martha said it all in many kinds of ways and very mysterious—it's something that just keeps you driving forward, questioning, demanding, not accepting except the ultimate at every level. Knowing what that ultimate is—knowing, discovering how to get at it.

BWM   *Is there anything that you are working on now that is that expression for you?*

CD   Yes. After making a film about, what I call, the personal poetics of a Martha Graham dancer, which is my experience of being a Martha Graham dancer with the same group of people that I worked with to make that film. We did a lot of filming of the technique, and these were all dancers that I had worked with over fifteen to twenty years. I am calling it Terpsikon, a dictionary of dance.

The kind of theatricality and physicality that is required to do Martha's work can also be brought to bear on other work. I have been able to bring my experience to younger choreographers who are not necessarily interested in Martha's repertoire but have in fact discovered the fundamental and the very powerful elements that make that a rich source for creating art and are interested in tapping into that. That has been for me fantastically exciting, to work with those artists and to watch them experience the work through my eyes and for me to experience their work. It has brought a lot of fresh thinking and challenges, which has been great as a performer.

BWM   Would you speak about your work in Mexico?

CD   The Graham technique was disseminated throughout the world and as far back as the 1960s. In the 1970s, by dancers who were teachers and went to other places and began to expand the work. So there were centers of interest. There was London, Israel, and there was Mexico. These were places who were committed to Martha's work who came to New York and they studied they brought back teachers. They brought back their own information, and they set off using the technique as their training model to build their own companies, their own repertoire, and styles.

One of the early tours in the late 1970s, we went to Mexico. I just fell in love with the culture, I loved the people, I loved what it was like to perform there, to work there, and the dance community was just wonderful, marvelous and generous and passionate. It has been a line through my work and my life ever since then, both personally and professionally. The qualities of the Graham work that interested those dancers and that community were qualities that I loved about the work: the dynamic, the power, the use of energy, the union of a personal expression with a physical medium, the willingness to work to a level that was exceptional and excessive and extraordinary.

When they first invited me and I first started teaching, I realized right away that there were many dancers, and this is true today—it is not different, who save all year long, sell candy on the street corner, give up food, take a bus, and stay in a hotel room with eight other dancers so that they can come and take your class. These are people who want to dance. They need to dance. They are there to soak up everything they can from what you are doing—that kind of passion, that kind of need, the way *that plays out in how they work in class. The expectations they have of themselves and the power that they generate is not unique to Mexico but it is where I discovered it. And I have been honored to be part of it for a long, long time in many different cities and many different companies.*

I often think that if Martha were looking down or up, she would be very excited to see that many men and women, hordes of people pounding their bodies, doing that movement, making it their own, being inspired by it, starting companies, starting schools—passing it on to another generation. She would recognize the power and the beauty and the absolute demand that they put on themselves. I think that she would also be happy to see the way that people use what they have gained working with the Graham work to make a contribution to their community.

I expect and want to believe that a significant part of the reason that contemporary dance is powerful is because it does address or give an outlet to important society, cultural, political questions. Some artists take that on as a purpose. "I am gonna do this antiwar, this is antiracism"—that is great, and some of the most wonderful things I have seen have been those kinds of works, sometimes done humorously, sometimes seriously. I think that is how modern dance began and how Martha's work began: as a reaction, like any artist, to what was going on in society a way to do something different, challenge yourself at the same time as communicating something to a community of people. We talk about self-expression. Self-expression is nice; it is not necessarily art, and I am not sure it is the goal. I am thinking that the communication of an important idea affecting people in different kinds of ways, provoking them, scaring them, inspiring them— that is more a goal. If you happen to be doing self-expression as well, that is great, but it is not the goal—something about important ideas in the world being expressed through dance.

BWM *There is often a criticism of modern dance with these emblematic leaders and chorus dancers who dress up to look like them. Not as self-expression, just mimicking—but those people are willing to acquiesce, perhaps, their individual self-expression in order to contribute to that greater expression ... something in there?*

CD *Again it is a perspective on art and how we learn art, how we do art. I do not know an art form that is not learned through apprenticeship, unless it is outsider and that is why it's called that (which I happen to love). But in general, any kind of art has an apprenticeship learning at some level from other people. And then you go on to break off on your own and do your own thing. I do not think there is a better learning experience than doing that. I cannot say that, it is not challenging.*

I can say that being in the chorus of most of Martha's repertory and then being a soloist in those same dances and in many cases being the

central figure in many of those—being in the chorus of Appalachian
Spring *and then the Bride in* Appalachian Spring *or being in the chorus of*
Diversion of Angels, *then dancing Red dancing Yellow. It is all learning. It
is all mastering your craft and feeling everything from the inside out and
carrying that to the next task. That might be part of what you were saying
about, Graham is not for everybody. It is kind of long form in my view,
and I like that, I like the depth of that. There is nothing more powerful
than being in a chorus and demanding—presenting and dancing together
for whatever the cause is. It is one of the things that is very beautiful about
my experience in Mexico. There is nothing more powerful. You go into
every little pueblo, every little town, and everybody is dancing together.
There is nothing more powerful, individually or communally.*

*There is room for both of those, the communal and the individual. It is
a little naive to somehow think that because you are in Martha Graham's
chorus or the Rockettes or a ballet company—because you are in a group
of people doing the same steps that somehow that is not personally
expressive or creative. I think that people's ideas about what actually
constitutes the art is very limited because that was certainly never my
experience.*

Artist, choreographer, and performer Javier Dzul is one of the dancers
who was touched by the Graham diaspora in Mexico. In his interview, he
speaks of the significance of Graham's work to him and the power of art to
transmute cultural boundaries.[6]

BWM   *What is your relationship to the Graham canon/legacy?*

JD   *I am the Artistic Director of Dzul Dance, which is a company that
uses circus, ballet, contortion, and different arts of movement to create
different styles* [of performance]. *The work is based on legends from
Mayan culture, history, and mythology because I am Mayan.*

*Graham was a very important part of my life, and I think that it
helped me to be able to communicate my work, which is based on ancient
traditions, to Americans. I live in America* [United States] *right now, and my
work basically, is always seen by Americans first and then everywhere else. In
the beginning I felt that my work was very raw, not good for these modern
people. I think in Graham, I learned so much about art and her perception
of art through the way she developed each piece. It really helped me, as a
creator, to develop my own work.*

*I studied at the Graham School from the time I was eighteen years old.
Before that, I studied in Mexico because Graham was, and it still is, a very
important technique. I studied at Ballet Nacional de Mexico and the school
in Xalapa, Veracruz; it was there I learned about Martha. Then I became a*

---

[6] Personal interview with Javier Dzul.

student here at the Graham School, and I danced with this second company, the ensemble. It was weird because at the moment that I got into the Martha Graham Company, the Company kind of disappeared and changed. I think it was good for me and also sad in many ways because during my whole youth, I really, really, really wanted to be a part of that company. Then suddenly everything changed, and it changed my life in a way. I mean it was very painful because I wanted to experience the work at that level.

But then somehow I think not being able to perform the work, not getting there 100 percent, forced me to create my own vocabulary.

BWM   *What was it about the repertory and/or the technique that spoke to you?*

JD   *I think it was the drama, the artistic representation of many things like The Chosen One for example in* Rite of Spring. *It is very, I could say, related to my culture because that happens in my culture. You get chosen, sacrificed, [made] to prove your[self] in your youth. So, to see the work and to see the body representing those moments and the Company representing those moments is so powerful. It is great to see that piece of art. That is important for me, and many other works as well. She was a genius. Everything teaches you something about relationships between people, with the world, and with yourself. It is very interesting that you can be able to create it, to see it, and to feel it.*

FIGURE 15 Rite of Spring. *Dancers: XiaoChuan Xie and Ben Schultz. Photograph by Paul B. Goode.*

BWM   *Is there anything that strikes you as cultural appropriation in* Graham's Rite of Spring?

JD   *Look, there is nothing in this world that has not been said. There is no movement that has not been done before. To believe that something belongs to someone is, I don't know, I don't think there's anything that belongs to anyone uniquely. You can find things in Mayan culture that you find in Chinese culture, that you find with the Persians and with the Greeks. You can say the Greeks came to the Mayan culture and took it but I think we as artists have a way that we communicate in some strange place that is not easy to express. There is something in the universe that connects art, and at some point, I think art, movement, ideas, and cultures somehow connect. We are universal. Sometimes when we go to other places we can communicate with other people even if we don't speak the language.*

You know, when I came here, I did not speak Spanish well, and I did not speak English. I spent one year [in New York], *and people thought about me like, "Oh this guy thinks he is very, very good" or "He is very awkward," but I did not know how to express myself. So I could not say anything, I could not say "yes" or "no." And the way that I learned was by opening myself and just listening. That was not easy in a way because sometimes when someone wants to explain something to you too much and you don't speak the language you get confused. When someone is very clear and shows you "I want this" and shows you, you do your best to get it. But when someone says, "I want this but ... this and this and this"* [indicates mixed messages], *then you get confused and wonder, "What does that person mean?" That is the case when you don't understand the language and that was very hard for me.*

But somehow I was able to communicate with people even though I did not understand the culture at all. So for me everything belongs to the universe and everybody, and as long as we are open to say this is art and this is my point of view of things and we don't think, "Oh this is me, this is only me." Art should connect the beauty of life—should connect the amazing aspects of being alive to other people.

BWM   *Graham has been quoted many times as saying that she didn't create anything, she simply revealed what was already there. Are there any Graham philosophies that resonate strongly with you?*

JD   *I think the Graham world absorbs you. When you are there as a student, the movement, the whole thing absorbs your being; it affects your perception of art, your perception of movement, and how you express yourself. I think the Graham dancer moves differently to any other dancer because of her point of view, of seeing art and the body as art; that makes the Graham dancer different to other dancers. If you see a company and* one of them is a Graham dancer, you're gonna know it, you're going to see it—you cannot hide that.

The philosophy, you can call it a philosophy, or the mark, stayed with me. So I cannot say that "I was not there," because you'll see it, the body cannot lie. You can't lie about where you're coming from, so, I think that's what I could say that I can see in myself.

BWM   Did studying and living in a body of work that came from a female body have any particular significance for you?

JD   When you have a great creator, [gender] doesn't exist, the male and the female. Those things are important because it's part of the history of the dance. For example, if we say this dance is about men or this dance is about women, you will see the difference [in movements]. But when you are a creator, when you create for women or men and the creator becomes both. When I create on my company for women, I am the women, and when I create for the men, I become the man so ... for me that's never been a problem. I remember as a student that the women would learn the male parts and the men would learn the female parts. We did that in Graham. You just didn't think, "Oh I'm being a woman." I didn't even think about it. You just do it because you enjoy the movement, you enjoy the drama, you enjoy the way that you are forcing your body and creating art. It's not political. I think art is beyond that. When you are there in the Graham world, you are beyond political ideas.

You know, something that I learned when I had girls, I learned how to treat women. Before I had a daughter, I never understood women, but now I am a father of three girls and see that they are who they are. They are beautiful because they have to be beautiful; they don't have to pretend or try. I hope every man can have a daughter, and then see what that is. It's something else.

BWM   What did you take away from your work with the Graham canon in terms of movement?

JD   It took so long for me to get it out of my body because I respect the work so much. When I started to create my own work, it would go back to her. I would go back to movements that were clearly coming from Martha. Then I said, wait a minute, you're doing this because you want to do your own vocabulary your own style, so what is that? And then I went back to being Mayan, it was really hard because the movement is smaller, and there's more articulation of the body, and I grew up with that, but I did not dance it on stage ever.

When I tried to teach it to my dancers, they could not do it. I had grown up with it, so it was easy for me to do, but my dancers said, "No,

I cannot I do that." So it took a lot of time for me to get Graham out of my body because I used it to create movement on the other dancers. It was easier for them to do [codified modern technique] than my vocabulary, which was harder for them. It would take too much time for them to learn it. Now, the longer I can keep dancers in the Company the more I could develop my style and my way of moving. Little by little, I started not to use any of the Graham work at all and to use only my movements.

My work is not only one thing. I started using lots of different styles and techniques like ballet, contortion, gymnastics—mixing things, and now my work is a mixture of everything. I feel free to say "I'm gonna do a pitch" [Graham pitch turn] or "I'm going to do a tilt" or a double pirouette. I just let myself go into it without stopping myself. It took time to get to that transition and saying, "Who am I, what am I?" and it came down to me excepting that I mixed already. I am in a mix of Mayan, Graham, ballet, circus performer, and accepting that, that's your work, is important.

BWM *Is there anything else that you would like to share about your experience in the Graham world?*

JD *I always remember when I went to school in Mexico, I did not speak Spanish, I only spoke Mayan. I learned about the Martha Graham technique and ... you know when you go to school, and they teach you something very important, like, they teach you ballet, you never imagine that that person [the creator of the technique] is alive. But when I went to school, I was young and I learned the [Graham] technique and was so in love with Graham; the technique and Company and thought about the School, and knew I wanted to get there.*

One day, I had a chance to go [to the Martha Graham School]. It was in the winter intensive, I was very young, I didn't speak English, and suddenly the door opened and there is Martha. And she was so full of light—so much light on her body! She was older, but just to see her, I was like "Damn, she's alive." For me it was like I was seeing a ghost. That I remember, it was very important for me to say, "Wow, she's alive." It gave even more importance to me being here. Because sometimes when you learn things from people who are not present or alive, it's a little bit more away from the root of where it comes from. But when you see the person is still there and you can get that light that she had ... I wanted to feed myself with that light, I wanted to get it on me.[7]

It is in this spirit of passing knowledge in lineage that I address the metaphysical space of regeneration where dancers begin their world anew. In its ninety-four-year (and counting) history, the Martha Graham

---

[7] Personal interview with Javier Dzul.

Dance Company has spawned many offshoots from choreographers who were either inspired to develop their own body of work or inspired by a component of her canon, such as the movement vocabulary or an imbedded physical idea such as rigor. For example, long-time collaborators in both the Martha Graham Dance Company and Buglisi Dance Theater (BDT), Christine Dakin, Terese Capucilli, and Jacqulyn Buglisi have spent decades unpacking, developing, and creating new works within the language of Graham's canon.

In 2010, Artistic Director of Buglisi Dance Theater and choreographer Jacqulyn Buglisi composed a site-specific ritual to be performed on September 11th of each year in remembrance of the 2001 terrorist attacks on New York City, Washington, D.C. and Flight 93 where thousands of lives were lost within minutes. Buglisi was compelled by a vision to create a galvanizing and transformative choreographic intervention. Buglisi's collaborators, Italian artist Rosella Vasta and costumer Christina Giannini, both contributed integral elements which bring design and symbolism into the dance ritual as much as the dancers' walks and gestural meditation. These elements of movement, design, and form function as part of a continuum of all sacred art and are centrally connected to Buglisi and her life's work within the Graham cannon.

Here, Buglisi, Artistic Director/Founder of Buglisi Dance Theater, Chair of Graham Division, The Ailey School/Fordham BFA program and principal dancer Martha Graham Dance Company 1977–89, shares her experience and how Graham has affected her as a choreographer. Speaking about the *Table of Silence*, Buglisi says:[8]

> We feel the heartbeat of humanity when we feel our own heart beat.
> The dancer like the poets, have to tell the truth.

BWM   *What is the* Table of Silence Project?

JB   *A ritual.*
   The Table of Silence Project 9/11 *represents the common threads of humanity which unite all mankind into a single force with common goals and aspirations regardless of race, culture, or religion. Celebrating the resilience of humanity, we honor justice and freedom for all people suffering systemic oppressions, through listening and compassion, a united moment of silence—a call to Action for Peace, in our world. Its mission continues to evolve, and this year [2020] I felt compelled with courage to create a reimagined TOS as an Awakening in response to the global pandemic and the Black Lives Matter movement for racial justice.*

---

[8] "My [Buglisi] works are often inspired by the writings of philosophers, scientists, historians, and poets: Michael Meade, Gibran, Rilke, and many more."

The Table of Silence Project *is a ritual, a multicultural prayer for peace in response to the shattering tragedy of 9/11. My vision is moving through and intimately woven from out my life experience, its challenges and from opening my heart to listen, to see how I may participate in what is in front of me. To be in service to the community; to be sensitively aware of what is before me and act as a messenger through my art. I hope that I am working responsibly in service to humanity. I believe as dancers, as choreographers, as human beings, some of us devote our lives to our work and its education, a lifelong process. "I practice dancing every day, the way I practice living."*

So it's not separated, and I don't know that I ever chose dance or it chose me. I think many of us are just born with this deep passionate urgency to dance. This need to take action through the physical body, a universal language that speaks about the human condition, the ordinary and the profound. The Table of Silence Project *for me was an answer to what was happening before, on and after 9/11; what happened at that catastrophic moment, during that time and just preceding, actually leading up to it. The unforgettable images of the ceremonial multitude of ghost-like people walking in silent motion, covered in white dust, up the West Side Highway. Throughout that year there were rumblings happening inside of me, an unexplained sense of foreboding, finding myself repetitively listening to Fauré's Requiem, an elegy. I believe we are all connected. We are part of the journey of humanity through the ancestral threads that bind us.*

Mythic stories, as metaphor may help us make sense of life's intimate meanings. "Through mythic tales we relate to the deepest part of ourselves while connecting to the greater imagination and universal truths." In times of chaos we need stories that bridge distances. Life is impermanent, like the constant ebb and flow of oceans. Just like Earth our bodies are fluid, we are water, we connect to the natural world. We surrender to the beauty and to the flow of life.

My vision for the Table of Silence Project *is borne out of Ancient Ritual. Scaffolding, layering, geometric patterns, and proportions are integral to crafting the formal architectural structure. The movement vocabulary and design stems from symbols that have deep meaning in ritual, such as the concentric circles and sacred geometry. The central circular Fountain gives us the symbol of the water for purity, and the continuity of the life cycle, important to the transcendent spiritual experience. Three concentric circles make a peace labyrinth manifesting the mandala's cosmic process of transforming the universe from suffering to joy. Sacred geometry revolving around the number 12 is core to the composition: the 12 points of the circle and 12 gestures each repeated 10 times by the dancers creates a mantra within the moving mandala for peace and harmony. Love is when we place our hand on our heart, and we feel the heartbeat of humanity; the Drum is the amplification of the heart beat; with each step we touch the sole of our foot to the soul of the* earth. We relate to symbols whether it's a rosary's repetition of prayers ten and one and ten and one and ten and one. It's the same when you recite a Sanskrit mantra using the one hundred and eight mala beads, the repetitions create inner focus concentration and illumination of the primordial sun.

The practice of repetition is important to the meditative quality, essential to creating a divine if you will ritual. To breathe together creates the physical awakening of the Human Spirit. As the dancers practice the 12 gestures in repetitions of 10 it becomes a movement mantra without being forced. Manifesting the mindful power of the breath allows us to transform the space into a sacred temple. If we don't have the balance of oxygen on our planet, there will be destructive change to existence as we know it now. Maybe this biblical COVID-19 is a warning. The ravaging of the resources of the earth and Indigenous ways of knowing are being destroyed on our planet. This is part of the evolution of the Table of Silence Project; it speaks to those issues of wars with each other, the natural world, systemic injustices, and oppressions facing us today.

The Table of Silence Project expresses what makes us human. It's message of peace and healing is far reaching and holds great relevance, in addition to the 9/11 commemoration. It strives to be a transformative experience that reveals the strengths, Truths and vulnerabilities of our collective society. The reimagining of the Table of Silence Project 9/11 in 2020 is a powerful message of awakening as we address the global pandemic and Black Lives Matter movement for racial justice. [It] honors all of those whose lives are impacted by the current crises individually and in our country, that we are facing now and across the landscape of the world so profoundly impacted by the story of racial inequity; the need for the stories that are threading through us, and the courage that it takes to make change. I always say that "life is a miracle therefore you are a miracle." We will get through this!

Co-Presented by Lincoln Center and Buglisi Dance Theatre, the re-imagined Table of Silence Prologue during the pandemic in 2020 featured twenty-eight compellingly courageous principal dancers maintaining the Labyrinth's three concentric circles, while manifesting a transcendent spiritual energy for healing and compassion, with a completely different compositional pattern. Led by John Ragusa and Pamela Fleming on conch and trumpet, and my artistic collaborators Terese Capucilli, Composer/Violinist Daniel Bernard Roumain performing The Loss and My Country interwoven with the spoken word by Mark Bamuthi Joseph in his unforgettable poem "The Awakening."

And again out of chaos comes the breath upon which love floats. Love floats. And again I am awakening.

—Marc Bamuthi Joseph, poet,
Reimagined Table of Silence Prologue (2020)

Staging a large scale site-specific dance is where the major virtue of having worked with Martha was a blessing. And of course the years growing up with my father, his designer and architectural sensibilities, and my loving to design on graphic paper.

And the gift of being close to Martha, my mentor ... For me, one of the most important privileges was to be able to sit in front of the room next to her during rehearsals. I was so honored to be included while she was still so masterfully choreographing. It was especially exciting because she needed us to interpret for her that physicality, and the electrifying energy she desired. Dancing for her and experiencing how she would create, most memorably Primitive Mysteries, *a ritual, profoundly influenced my journey as a choreographer. It was very, very beautiful in its structure and the way it revealed that simple ritual, timeless and resonating.*

When you create a ritual it brings together many different elements, most important for me is the human story, the dancers, and the artistic collaborators. It's about the deep story inside bursting to be told. That is coming from opening the self, opening the channels to being vulnerable to feel, to see what is there.

[It is] inside the marrow, the blood memory, the DNA, the bones; and having been absorbed in Graham technique since I was thirteen and then teaching it for over fifty years. It lives inside your skin and in your heart and in your soul.

It's more for me, explorative mining and improvisation than it is choreographic devices that we learn in composition. I always felt like I had to let go of that. The language of dance is organic to me; crafting and creating dances has been a lifelong fulfilling mission. Rendering one's message is not easy. Dance as a world unto itself where the divine realm, the metaphysical, and reality converge; where a mystery of some great poem can be excavated. My work is multi-layered and reveals itself in the process of spontaneous creative exploration. Opening the channels is what Martha would say one can learn from being still.

Art is a powerful igniter of awakening inspiration and hope during times of crisis and darkness as well as celebration. I feel it is a time for deep introspection, compassion, and grace, and the need for reconciliation and understanding having the courage to make change for the resilience and hope of our thriving future. The Table of Silence Project *over these ten years has become a movement for peace, bridging boundaries with all nations. Putting out our hands and asking how to participate in what was before us, I continue to feel the need for the call to action for peace, personally and globally. The* Table of Silence Project *is a re-birth. Like the phoenix rising from the ashes, we never give up.*

As long as there exists humanity, there exists the need for dance.
                                                              —*Jacquelyn Buglisi*

Transgression

The image in Figure 16 is a perfect illustration of performance artist Richard Move's decades-long body of work investigating and presenting truncated interpretations of Graham's most iconic dances. Symbolism is reimagined in the Noguchi-esque set from *Errand into the Maze*; a phallus shoots up from the ground while the vaginal opening is wrapped up tight with a snake guarding its entrance. Richard Move as Graham holds the dagger from Clytemnestra's "knife dance" in a fierce elongated contraction/hinge/knee crawl which is the essence of Graham's technique. This hyper-loaded picture presents a concentration of forms and an overt sexuality encompassing everything there is to love about Graham.

FIGURE 16 *Richard Move as Martha Graham. Photograph by Andrew Hetherington for* Interview.

Richard Move, PhD is a performer, choreographer, Artistic Director of MoveOpolis!, and Assistant Arts Professor at New York University, Tisch School of the Arts. Starting in the 1990s, Move gained acclaim for channeling Martha Graham in spirit and demeanor in his nightclub act, *Martha@ Mother*. Once a month, Move as "Martha" would host the elite performers of New York's postmodern dance scene framed by his versions of Graham's most famous chorus works. I had the thrill of being one of those chorus dancers. In Move's interview below, he speaks to the sex politics of gender identity and the role of feminism in both Graham's and his artistic practices.

BWM   *What of Graham's persona, body of work, and/or philosophy activated agency for you in your performance life, either as Martha Graham or in another way?*

RM   *First and foremost, the combination of the power she's held over me has been a philosophical one that is transgressive in so many ways. And then what kind of really ensconces me within the philosophy and the transgression is the physicality. In terms of gender, it's only in the last five or ten years that we have even had terms that were floating out there in the world. But I know I have always felt that gender was fluid, that my identity was fluid. And so I think that I am able to in that way more readily access her than others who do not have fluidity. Accessing what she refers to or we might categorize as woman. Whether it's a woman's point of view in one of the ballets or what a woman can achieve and do—a woman's revenge and what not. I feel like that is very close to me, I can access that. Again, I do think it's philosophical and then somehow the philosophy gets activated physically through the movement and through the performance. And for me when I mean movement/performance I also mean voice and text that I write based on her readings, as you know, because that's obviously a very physical event.*

So I think she took a hold on me in that way. I think there were a bunch of confluences. Right when I moved to New York, I finished at VCU [Virginia Commonwealth University] *and the summers at ADF* [American Dance Festival], *she died. It was that moment when the greats pass, it sends a shockwave even if you're not involved with them. I remember her death was such big news even though none the people around me were connected. And then at that time I found myself at the Robert Fitzgerald studio here in New York on the Upper West Side just filled with great Graham dancers: Yuriko Kimura, Yuriko Kikuchi, Ken Topping, Maxine Sherman,* [Katherine] *Crocket, that's how and where we met, Jennifer Bindford was there too. I got to know them.*

Basically, I was with them all through the 1990s and he [Robert Fitzgerald] *died early 2000s, I think he died 2002.*

So this was a really interesting moment. I had just arrived in New York, I was very involved with downtown performance and a certain aesthetic.

Yes downtown performance is what you'd call it working with Dancenoise, Pooh Kaye, different, more experimental choreographers yet somehow finding myself in that environment of Robert's studio—loving it, the beauty of that pain.

Then, being surrounded by these greats, all the women that I was referring to, except Ken and Mario Camacho. There was an intensity at that moment when I started with him—when she passed, they were so close. I would go [to Robert Fitzgerald] *in the evenings. I was often his last* [Pilates] *appointment of the day because I was working at night in clubs and things. So I would always make the last appointment, so sometimes it would just be he and I or maybe one person finishing up. He would tell me stories about Graham and he would give me little gifts that she had given him. He even had some radio interviews on old cassette tapes that he would play. And so I got very turned on by hearing about her, learning about her and also her will* [power].

He was describing how she had had appointments with him right up until her death, literally a few weeks before, and by the last few years it sounds, they wouldn't do much but they would sit and talk. And for some reason, Ron [Protas], *it was the only place that Ron would kind of leave her alone without the nurse or him or Chris Herman or somebody else kind of babysitting. I guess because they had such a long relationship, he thought it was safe just the two of them. So they would sit and talk, and it was one of the only places she had that kind of freedom.*

He described something in her early 90s where she could still lie on her back and kick her left leg over her head. She was trying to do ronde de jambs on the Cadillac with the feet in the straps and the springs, and was struggling so hard and shaking and forcing her body that she projectile vomited all over the mirrors and was so ashamed and embarrassed, but still, like railing against that body. And all of that is so inspiring and fascinating and interesting and devastating and sad. Because then you think, oh my gawd, the hands and feet were riddled with arthritis at that point. At that point she would have been off the stage for twenty-five years already. You'd think you could accept and embrace going into that part of your life if you've accomplished that much—but not so. All of that was just fascinating and just fed my desire to experiment with that first performance in 1994 and then two years later realizing that it was too rich not to explore regularly. So, yeah, it was that confluence of events—my arrival here, studying there, her death, and the fact that she was withheld from me. I felt like I missed something. I felt like I really missed something.[9]

And what I mean by that is … I don't know if there has ever been a dancer as tall as me in the Company. That would have been a problem. Also I was quite effeminate, I never would have been cast in the Company. All

---

[9] At the time of Move's early dance education many college programs rejected the formality of Graham's technique.

that was fine. That's not what I meant by I was missing something. What I meant by that was to maybe have experienced the technique. I guess by the time I was in high school, she wasn't teaching at all. To experience studying that technique, I missed out on that but kind of made up for it by going to performances and stuff and seeing the work. So I feel like she was withheld and something compelled me to start my own research in this very strange, unusual way. For me it was never about being in the Company; it wasn't even a desire. You know that would never happen.

I was wishing I had been trained like that, I could fucking do the things that Maxine was doing in the Pilates studio and on stage. That's because of Graham and ballet so there was that technical thing and then this obsession with the person again, married to the physical. There was something about working the body from the inside out from the center outwards in Robert's studio while he told stories and/or old cassette tapes of interviews with her. Something about her voice, her words, her thoughts. All of that was really compelling.

Mind you, I was the only one thinking this way. Nobody in my scene was thinking about Graham. They thought I was crazy going all the way to the Upper West Side when I lived on Avenue B, for Pilates. Certainly when we were doing Jackie 60 and I was performing with Dancenoise at PS 122 and also Pooh Kaye and Mark Dendy at the Joyce, the Kitchen, nobody was discussing Graham. Now some little things I remember, Lucy Sexton when Agnes's [DeMille] book came out, she was reading it when I was reading it, so there might have been a little chat but not in a deep way. And then it was just everyone was shocked and every dance person would say, "Can you believe Graham died," but I was really going deeper down the rabbit whole.

So that's when the personality started to take over—her personality started to take over and really consume me. And then from that first show, as I was doing that first show, I understood that we were onto something long term. It was palpable. And that it was fulfilling some need. There was a need for Bertram Ross, rest his soul, to be in that audience and to tell me afterwards "your lipstick needs to be a darker red" or for Stuart [Hodes] then to come and perform. Yuriko [Kikuchi] to coach us a little bit, for Linda [Hodes] to be deeply involved.

The great meaning, it had to be, even in this strange way, to be revisiting the amazing biography of that life. Thinking about different contributions all along the way, relishing in the fact that she is the mother of it all. It's almost (it's kind of a funky term) but it was almost a "safe space" for people to appreciate. And when I say was, I mean specifically that space of Mother[10] and four or five years there. And then it's continued but that was so concentrated, one venue a show every month or every three or

---

[10] *Martha@Mother*, the nightclub act.

*four months—that kind of thing. And then for people like Mark Morris
to be thinking again a little bit about Graham when he participated
and made new solos for the series. You know and [Paul] Taylor gave us
Epic, that beautiful solo that Sharon Kinney did at Town Hall. Anyway
the list goes on then, young choreographers may be thinking about her
for the first time. That's something that's been very consistent. Very
often when I go places with the show, I fully expect people to ask for
biography recommendations or further reading and research type things.
That's been very meaningful because so much of dance knowledge is
transmitted body to body and orally and physically like that. So for me
to be transmitting this knowledge in this way makes sense for a dance
artist—to be transmitting this knowledge orally and physically and through
performance—I think makes sense.*

BWM   *She was so literate and a huge part of her life as an artist was
intellectual. Speaking and writing, articulating her thoughts in words.*

RM   *Yes, and I never felt that anybody else has come close to that. I
always felt and do very much to this day that that's an integral part of
being an artist. And for some reason, maybe because dance was disparaged
and is disparaged, in say my upbringing—not a legitimate career path and
that kind of thing. I almost felt like somehow I had to overcompensate for
the intellectual rigor, and somehow she did that very well for me. And I
feel like I still have to prove that to this day. I am turning my head now to
my syllabi for next semester. Thinking, "These are great dancers but they
need to value their learning, their intellectual journey, and their writing
and thinking and writing dance." (Her)story as I call it. I don't know that I
have quite woken them up to that yet.*

BWM   *In your opinion, would you imagine that Graham was aware
and conscientious of the impact of her philosophies in terms of being a
visionary and creating something for generations of dancers to build upon?
She created something that we will continue to live into and her words are
an integral component.*

RM   *I think so. She thought of the philosophy, the text. I think it's one
of the reasons I love that 1963 interview so much, because for seventy-five
minutes, the physical is married and it becomes clear how inseparable it is
from the philosophy, from literature. That all taps into these essentials and
universals in human nature in a very sustained way. For me as a performer,
I enter and don't leave until it's over seventy minutes later. But also I think
for the audience, because in the variety show format you have breaks
from that, but there is no break [in the 1963 interview]. And similarly I
think you get it more from that interview than from even going to see the*

*Graham Company because you are with her with her words and thoughts
for so long. You know it's about that intensity of time and how deep
they go. Yes, and I feel like that's missing with a lot of choreographers.
I'll read interviews occasionally and think, "Oh that's not so rich." Or
I'll hear somebody speak and secretly I'll say to myself, "Oh, I wish they
were more articulate about what they're doing." So she's really the gold
standard of that.*

BWM   *Marrying the physical and the philosophy, the House of the Pelvic
Truth …*

RM   *How do I relate to that without a uterus?* [laughter]

BWM   *Well, no, because there are people with a uterus who don't
connect with it.*

RM   *It's beyond the uterus because it's the ultimate body–mind
connection. That's kind of what we were saying about her marriage, this
happy marriage, this melding, this inseparability of thought, philosophy,
deep intellectual investigation, and rigor married to this intense physicality
that we've never seen before, and that some people can't physically handle.
But I have always wondered what it would be like to have a uterus and a
vagina and do the work. I imagine there is connection that is profound.
And I see it in you [BWM], [Katherine] Crockett, and some other people
too. I've always seen that, which is why I always feature the women. I
mean she always featured the women too, but you know what I mean. I do
think that there is an affinity there that is uterus dependent.*

BWM   *Thinking about the concept of the contraction.*

RM   *Orgasm. If we are just speaking in base physical terms, to me
that would be the most direct route. That orgasm is a direct physical
way that all people can at least intellectually latch onto. It's that deep,
it's that primordial, that physical. And I do think the nerve endings are
involved. There is an ecstatic quality to it for sure. I wonder too if maybe
some people are fearful of the technique because it is so wonderfully,
overtly sexual. And then the content of so many of the ballets is [sexual].
So I've wondered if some people just kind of shy away from that biography
in the classroom. What would it be like for a parent of a teenage girl to see
in one of those classes?*
     *And then there's a religiosity to it as well that I think is super important,
the ecstasy of that connection with this higher self. The profundity of it
is this union of the higher self, the more animal self, the intellectual self,
the primordial self, the cultivated self, the self that is already there in the
epigenetics of the body. All of that kind of blood memory, I think we tap*

into through exploring what a contraction is.

It was interesting you brought up Cunningham. I don't think we would be as attracted to it if the Graham torso weren't on it and that if he [Merce himself] *hadn't understood that so deeply. Because that was in his body profoundly. I don't know if all of that could have worked without his acute understanding of that and his acute understanding of drama. I'm paraphrasing, but he understood that it was human nature ... you put a body onstage and then another body joins and we're already attaching a narrative to it. He innately understood that, and so his ballets are very narrative in their own way because that's human nature. And I would say the same with an object. If there's a solo moment in Rainforest with a balloon, there is a little inherent drama there too. I think when it's 2000 and you're Merce Cunningham, to be speaking deeply about Graham is a testimony to the imprint right. And Yvonne[11] too—it's almost like those are fresh wounds. So that could be interesting.*

I spoke at Juilliard about gender and casting and this notion of classics came up. And it was really interesting to think about. One of the topics that came up was what do we do with the classics and gender? I used Graham's Appalachian Spring *and* Agon, *the very cis-gendered heteronormative partnering, I brought those two up because I thought they'd be iconic of those gender norms. I think I disappointed some of the students because I basically said, it's not our place to put two women in* Appalachian Spring. *I don't think they would necessarily do anything differently now just because we have the language. I don't feel like that brings it into the present day necessarily.*

And Terese [Capucilli] *made this point and one of the other faculty as well. This notion that there are other pieces that can have a fluidity. And it was interesting because Rite of Spring came up, I guess Juilliard students learned that last year, so it has been in the Juilliard atmosphere. Terese seemed to be open to this notion of some different casting choices but then ultimately felt that women would not necessarily be strong enough to do the partnering and lifting, which I can totally see. Then a young Juilliard student, a woman said, "Well we're not trained to do that," so the student was expressing this notion of, well, if we trained to partner everyday, we certainly could. Really interesting.*

My point is that I don't think that you can have a man or even a non-binary person as The Chosen One. That's uterus bound, that's about giving birth in my opinion. And Martha's not here to ask, so I feel like we need to leave it. Something about contextualizing or bringing into the present where I think we need to be a little more reserved, i.e., no reason to jump on the bandwagon and have a non-binary person performing as The Chosen One. Maybe if there is a strong enough woman, send a woman out with the men for the chorus in that particular ballet.

---

[11] Post-modern choreographer, Yvonne Rainer.

When you look at the Bride in Appalachian Spring, *that's about birth as well. The promise of fertility and birth, so I think that shouldn't be tampered with. There are certain things with the repertory that I don't think should be tampered with. Some things are of their time, and that is a beautiful thing. I don't agree that an audience can't sit through an evening of* Clytemnestra. *There's durational viewing now, people are into durational performance. They can see Taylor Mac for twenty-four hours, they can see three acts of* Clytemnestra. *And then offer other alternatives for other parts of the season. So I don't know that that's a way to bring it into the present more. I think its about a balance, and I think Janet has found some nice balances. Like* Lamentation Variations, *where we are reflecting on the past in a very presentist way. So I think that's a good thing. But I do think some aspects need to be off limits too.*[12]

Sharing in Community

Movement Migration is "a collective of seasoned dance artists collaborating to create and perform dynamic and poignant dance works that portray the depths of the human experience; the dances are shared with audiences locally and globally in performance and educational venues."[13] It's Artistic Director and Associate Professor of Dance at the University of North Carolina at Charlotte, Kim Jones, founded the collective in 2017. She danced in the Martha Graham Dance Company from 2001 to 2006.

BWM   *What was your inspiration in founding Movement Migration? Its artists are willing to go to a deep emotional place in their dance. How did you come choose your collaborators?*

KJ   *I created Movement Migration in 2017 in response to the 2016 presidential election in the United States of America. I felt that places and spaces for people with diverse beliefs and diverse backgrounds were being limited. I wanted to gather like-minded artists to work collaboratively on the processes of making dances and to share ideas with audiences around the world through conversation and hopefully performance.*
   I was lucky to find seasoned artists and educators who spanned three to four decades in age. These artist came primarily out of the modern dance and ballet canons. They came to Charlotte, North Carolina, for rehearsals and we began making dances collaboratively.

BWM   *How do integrate or relate your history, community, and work within Graham's artistic canon to that of Movement Migration?*

---

[12] Personal interview with Richard Move.
[13] Movement Migration, https://movementmigration.org/about.

KJ   *Many of the dancers come from the Martha Graham legacy and also from the José Limón legacy. There is something about the understanding of the body in space, the expressive body, the use of breath, the reverence of place, of where we stand. There is an understanding of the opposition from the soles of the feet to the top of the head in relation to the earth into the sky. So that when we move, we are moving with the space.*

There is an understanding of people's stories and the human condition. The training from the Graham School is so beautiful; it has a timeless beauty that is not of the past nor the future.

BWM   *What is significant to you about the name of your company, Movement Migration?*

KJ   *I always say, "Move to live, migrate to survive." Bodies and nature must move, wind must flow through space for seeds to be dropped into the soil. Movement must exist in the womb for the child to be born. Movement, for people who are aging, is going to help them to live a more full life. Movement brings circulation and flow, and with that comes migration. We, as people, migrate across lands for survival.*

I do not understand why some people want to let others die on massive scales. Why is it unsettling for so many people to help other people? Why is it okay to take someone's land and not honor what has been done there before? How can I live on this piece of land when I know that it has been taken from another group of people? Why not share it? All of those questions are important to me in educating and bringing awareness to the students who I am teaching at the university level. It is also important for me to continue to travel so as to bring people to unknown spaces that are different for them. It is important for people to find similarities and also appreciate differences.

When Movement Migration was created, we were dealing with a president who was set on building a wall between the US and Mexico, which was unsettling to me on so many levels. We do not all have to assimilate to get along. We should migrate to different spaces, take a look into other people's cultures, and learn to respect that their way is their way; it doesn't have to be your way.

BWM   *What are the major influences that you have received from your work within the Graham canon?*

KJ   *The discipline of the technique was so important in forming myself as an artist. This particular work spoke to me because I was able to access emotional content. Any strife that I may have been experiencing, I could put it into the work. Through repetition, I was able to lose the sense of being only myself in the work. It built my confidence and I was able to develop my own expression, which was already there; it helped me to channel my expression.*

Being in the Company, amongst people who are dedicated, its the rigor that helped raise the bar for me. There was a beautiful commitment in that company during the years I was there. A commitment to reaching for the highest good, whatever that was in the moment. It was a family with an amazing work ethic. There was a lot of sharing, which is often times antithetical to what people outside of the Company might believe. There was a lot of sharing of generational knowledge and a willingness and openness to bring our life experiences into our bodies in space.

We really supported one another and sensed that support on stage. We would watch each other from the wings every single night even if it was the same repertoire. I felt other dancers' energy as positive and intense in the sense of doing something really beautiful for ourselves and for the people. And it really made me accountable. The intensity of the group work brings forth a force which is stronger than the individual. That kind of work has built so many strong leaders. A beautiful thing about being in the Martha Graham Company are the many beautiful leaders who have come out of that body of work. It doesn't matter if you rose within the ranks in the hierarchy. I think it taught us never to give up, to never give up and to never lose hope. It pushed us to try—try to never lose hope, try to never give up. I feel it in my veins, the work is in my breath, it is in my pelvis, in my back, in my spiral release to the sky.

I am hoping that Movement Migration will push me to grow to be a better human being. I hope it will encourage myself and other people to listen more, to collaborate more, to build bridges, and to stay open-minded.

I created a virtual school during the pandemic [2020–1] that had over three hundred students from around the world and employed over thirty dance teachers. That is a testament to Movement Migration's expansion beyond the modern dance community. I am trying to be gentle with myself in the development of Movement Migration and not feel the pressure of hitting some kind of diversity chart checklist. Let's see what diversity really means to me in practice as a person of color in this country [United States]. I want to allow myself to grow and permit myself to make mistakes, to unlock new spaces at any level. I hope to inspire more people to open up spaces that may have been closed before because of awareness and fear of other people's judgment.

Looking at it from a director's lens, I allow people to come with their strengths as they are but also to try something new. Most of us [dancers] are mature artists [ranging in age from] 30s and 50s. There are not many places for mature dancers to be presented [in performance]; it's just not happening. It is uncommon for presenters to book dancers who are fully embodied in their middle-age years, but we are doing that and it is really beautiful.[14]

---

[14] Personal interview with Kim Jones.

Artistic Diaspora

In addition to the most iconic companies to come out of Graham's artistic lineage, Merce Cunningham and Paul Taylor, other companies were spawned either directly or indirectly by Graham and/or her influence. Because Graham had successfully developed a new method for dancing in the United States, her success was used as a template for different companies internationally. In the 1960s, she was invited by her patron Bethsabée de Rothschild to become an artistic advisor to the then newly formed Batsheva Dance Company in Tel Aviv, Israel. Graham sent her long-time and trusted principal dancer, Linda Hodes, to teach the Graham technique and stage Graham's repertory. In her book *Martha Graham's Cold War*, author Victoria Phillips writes on the subject:

> As the company found its footing, critics cited the professionalism of the Israeli dancers and called for Batsheva to be made a part of the permanent state apparatus. While Graham's works were the repertory core, and Hodes became instrumental, Rothschild had her own agenda: after having performed great international works, the Israelis would make their own.

> (176)

Batsheva Dance Company of Israel has become the most influential and sought-after contemporary dance company in the Western dance world under the direction of Ohad Naharin (who also danced in the Graham Company). His Gaga method (like Graham's) also revolutionized the world of contemporary dance.

Looking at the phenomenon of Ohad Naharin's Gaga method for training I find several commonalities and continuances from the Graham lineage as well as complete divergences. The connection between Gaga and Graham is found in cultivating sensitivity to those urges which motivate you. Where Graham is will based, Gaga is sensory based. Both ascribe an intelligence to the flesh, blood, and bones—listening to the body in space and through feeling.

Graham's art is also alive and well in France as documented by Raphael Molina who studied at the Martha Graham Center and has founded a concern called *Graham for Europe*. His social media platform galvanizes the Graham community living in Europe and presents research surrounding the global reach of her artistic diaspora. In his interview he describes the variety of cultural forces at play in Europe as related to teaching and learning within the Graham dance canon.

BWM   *Why did you start* Graham for Europe?

RM   *People especially in France perceive Graham as something old school and they do not see the connection of being Graham-trained and having a career. I did not want to have that gap between how I saw it as great for me and it could be great for other people and how it was perceived in general. I thought the first thing I could do is stop pretending nothing is happening* [with Graham] *in Europe.*

What if there was a platform showing that there are already things happening [in Europe with Graham training] *and destroy that self-fulfilling prophecy* [that there is no Graham in Europe]? *I didn't want to get caught in that. I was seeing a huge potential.*

The most important thing is that you connect. When you say the Graham community in Europe, there is not a sense of a community but we already are a community. We [practitioners] *do not talk because we are in different countries or do not come from the same generation. However, through New York, we actually are part of the* [Graham] *community. So I had to go and contact people in person. The moment you go and talk to them or take their class, it becomes very easy.*

It's not like New York where [the Martha Graham Company] *is part of the identity of the city. In France you have such a strong history of ballet and ballet is the norm. Globally, also, ballet is the norm. You have on one side the ballet world and on the other side the contemporary world that was not built with Graham; it was built against Graham. People wanted to go away from formal techniques. Only Alwin Nikolai and Merce Cunningham from the United States came through big institutions and were able to have a big impact on the French contemporary dance scene. But it moved away from an intense dance training.*

My generation in conservatory took ballet and contemporary. My contemporary training was influenced by release [technique] *and a little bit of Cunningham, but every teacher had a different class. I did not know that my own teachers were trained in New York and London in Graham and in Limón. I had no clue because they did not talk about it. I never had formal technique, and I was not able to identify them, but I was still some how part of that training. Even so, my contemporary dance still came somehow from American modern dance technique.*

Sometimes something is not a part of your history (and that's okay) or your country's history. And sometimes it is part of it but it is not the story people tell. You can never say that history is neutral. When I started teaching, that is when I saw all the issues that you face. A Graham teacher in a country far from New York is going to face a lot of resistance and you are not prepared. Only the field will give you enough experience.

I thought I have to do this research project. What resources are out there to help me as a Graham teacher in an environment that might not be the same as the people who taught me or the teacher I had fifteen years ago? What is going to help me? The technique has been documented, and it is still alive through the generations. But what I want to know is, when you teach, what really happens? What's going on and what happens in different spaces and times? Was it helpful or not?

How come the Batsheva Dance Company grew in that direction? How come England has disappeared, kind of? So, in pure pedagogy, what is the goal of education? Dancers being able to take that as a tool but not being restricted by it.

Geographically it looks like diaspora all over the place. Historically it went through so many phases. It's the same but not the same. Is it rich enough, that transmission? Even if you go far from New York, even if you were never in the Graham Company, what can it really give birth to? And also the question of freedom. Do we have a place? Is there room for a new generation to do something with it? What is the legitimacy for different people to teach?

I wanted to have those two big Graham extensions the UK and Israel, and then I was interested in going to the [Maurice] Béjart School[15] because theirs was a specific and unique thing. Another genius of the dance world [Béjart] decided to put Graham in his training. At Juilliard you get it, it's in the identity. She co-created the [studies there], it's in New York, but Béjart is far away [from the source]. They [students of Rudra] have ballet and Graham every day, six days a week, eleven months a year, two years—super intense. How is that going on?

How can you be trained as a Graham dancer there or in France at the Course Arts de Superior or in the UK through the Cohan[16] legacy? I was surprised everywhere I went. Witnessing a Graham class, a Juilliard was an experience, just that. Then of course it is Terese, but just watching that class, it was different. It was not the same Graham—you can see what it is to be in New York to be in a training that always had Graham to have beautiful dancers. At the same time, they are not trying to be Graham dancers. What does that mean? They are using Graham, but it is not a goal in itself.

In Israel, I didn't realize how intense the Graham legacy was—that they performed so many pieces of Graham and that she went there many times. And she was not the same as she was in New York. People don't perceive Graham in Israel the same way they do in the US. Again, it stayed in New York; in Israel it kind of evaporated. It was codified already when they got it. They went into other directions; they were on a different adventure clearly. That was a huge exchange, but the goal was not to have another Graham Company or to have a Graham-based company. The goal was for Israel to be a country on the map. Just like Graham, first she wanted to have American dance. What is American dance?

Sometimes part of the work is to say what history got told. As many stories as you can tell the better that people will be able to pick from it and choose. But it's very dangerous the moment you start having an official story. The double legacy in the UK—it was clear that it was Graham, but

---

[15] Rudra.
[16] Sir Robert Cohan.

it was Cohan, so it was another thing. He started calling it the Cohan method, but for us it's Graham. But for them, they got it from someone who is alive, still in the UK who was not put as a legend as Martha Graham. So they had more freedom, and they talk about practice, which is more encompassing than class or training or Graham technique.

Béjart again, such beautiful training, and it is a different Graham. So it raises many questions: What is the essence of that work? Why do we do it? Graham for Europe and my research project was about having some tools so we can talk about stuff instead of having all of those myths and behaviors that are reproduced and no one really knows.

I have written a thesis. I analyzed all of the interviews; I had thirty interviews in five countries. It touches on a lot of different things because the moment you talk about pedagogy and the work of these people, then it is about history, geography, sociology, economy, politics, and it is all intertwined. You cannot really separate the work of an artist or a teacher from all the conditions and all of the cultures of the people. It's just impossible.

I analyzed on an individual level, I did typologies of different Graham teachers schematically of course. Just like when you read your horoscope. I put different categories of teachers according to what I look at to show that actually there are so many different types of Graham teachers. How they inherited it, the natural inheritor, the sacred inheritor, the double inheritor. And then on a macro level is the context in which people teach. I can do an analysis of the French context in general, or in New York I really separate different phases of development. In Israel again so that people have a sense of how, when you contextualize something, you see that history has a depth. It is not just Graham is one thing. It's like, in this moment with these people, Graham was like that. And then you understand so many things. Or in Israel the [dancers] were coming through London, through The Place legacy.

Back then [1950s–1960s], you didn't have to go to New York to learn Graham and to appreciate it and to teach it. It was in a lot of places, people were able to experience it as a common practice. Today it is a different thing. If you don't go to New York, what can you really do with Graham? But, it is like a dead language and it can come back to life.

Now you have it in the biggest institutions, the Paris Opera School. Somehow it survived some places where you least expect it. Sometimes within a big institution it remains, and maybe it's more dogmatic and conservative, but it is a big institution; it can go through different decades and still be there because it is anchored, it is institutionalized. For Juilliard to get rid of Graham or the Paris Opera School (since 1993 they have had it) or for Alvin Ailey it would take a lot. If since the beginning of your school (like Juilliard or Ailey) you had that, then it is a big step to decide to take it out. So it survives in some places. The Paris Opera School, for example, back then they wanted to bring in some technique and it was Horton or Graham, and Nureyev was like Graham because he loved Graham and he used to go and perform with her. It's now 2021 and Iris Florentiny just took over the position [teaching Graham].

It is really what Martha Graham represented. It is hard for us to imagine, women didn't have a bank account. She created all of that, helped by other people of course. It was collaborative but she was the creative force. It's not like people were talking about vaginas; we didn't talk about it. To imagine that she released and based an entire technique on that [moving from the pelvis].

Maybe I can say something personal: of course going to New York and seeing all of the repertory, I saw that it was a female-centered company and repertory. For me it was cool because, even if I am a man, I already live in a lot of contexts where it is always male centered. It felt good to be somewhere where, why not?

When you understand that she is telling the story of this myth and she's going to say what she wants with it. Anytime you tell a story, it's never the real story. She's going to have a perspective on the story, that's what all artists do. Even if you want to do the authentic story, who knows! She's going to get into psychology and always putting those female figures. It's fascinating because she never said, "I am a feminist." She never said, "I am political." But what she was doing in the 1920s and 1930s was super political. She was able to push boundaries to create something new. To give space for a group of women to then be famous in the whole world. That is extremely political. What I discovered and didn't know is what happened in the 1960s and 1970s when she stopped being onstage and the center of that creative work because she wasn't necessarily always performing her choreographies and creating through her body—that is the moment when she, consciously or unconsciously, started becoming very institutionalized and becoming the norm in the US. She performed at the White House, and universities would teach Graham, and her Graham became more balletic.

The dancers were ballet trained, and also she [began to] *incorporate so much from ballet* [into her work]. *Ballet was the norm and ballet has a canon. We all know that's what a ballet dancer is. So somehow she was able to do that work that other people usually do when the artist dies. She was making it more acceptable for institutions, and some former dancers would say, "Oh, she's betraying," but that is also a natural course of things.*

Of course when you are thirty or forty [years old], *and there isn't any American modern technique known in the whole world, there is a lot to do. Then you do it, then you get old. How do you survive? I don't think she was a teacher in the way we might think, meaning someone who loves to be in the classroom teaching. I think she taught because she was training people. Just like when you have a guru, the guru is just doing his thing. So that part of the teaching, the amazing inspiration and pushing people to get something out of them and to help them become themselves through Graham to become an artist. She was doing that but not in a scholarly manner. To noble-ize Graham.*

My research was not about that but those were things that I read that helped me understand why teachers like Marnie Thomas or Robert Cohan, when they talk about Graham, for them, it is a really different thing from Janet [Eilber] or Peggy [Lyman]. What happened in between [generations] was that the ballet-influenced, institutionalization part of Graham [overtook the part that was] something revolutionary and not preservable so that it could be used by institutions to restrict bodies and tell them, "If you want to be professional, then this is what you have to do." Just like, "If you have ballet, then you will become a professional." I don't think in the 1930s people were saying, "Go study with Graham, you will become a professional." That was not the thing. Graham technique was not considered as one way to be legitimate. But then in the 1970s and 1980s, that was the case. The dance world has changed a lot since back then.

That is why I loved when she was in Israel with the Batsheva, if felt like they were coming from the Kibbutz and they were coming from different countries, they were all immigrants. I feel like it was those women who were working all day and coming to Graham in the evening, were not paid a dime and were throwing themselves in falls onstage like crazy! I was like wow!

It's not like in the 1970s when they learned Graham at Juilliard, very well trained, crème de la crème, beautiful dancers who came to work with a legend and they go there and yes, she is still creating and active but it is not the same revolution. Because you cannot! You have already revolutionized. So then you have Merce Cunningham, etc.

But going back to what become possible through Graham, which could be a very feminist thing [speaking about the ethics of transmission]: One of the things that I love about Graham is the power it gives you. How is it possible for people to think, "Oh you have a contraction and release, spiral in the body," which are there of course, but one thing it can give to young students is, "This is your body, this your life." It is a system that was created with many people and it has evolved. But really, the core of it is she was formulating. You are using dance, but the goal is never to do dance. The good dancer isn't a dancer, it is someone who makes you feel something. The goal is to have YOU do ... whatever you want. If feels like with the repertory there is always space.

It is about you and if it doesn't give you any power, go away. You shouldn't try to be something for someone else. She empowered many, many people. Many women and that is something super important.

The original intent she was preparing people to become artists and to be larger than life on stage. Which means you can be larger than life in life! When I compare it to ballet, that is what I love about Graham. As much as ballet has changed, you can still see and feel that it came from the king and the court and the hierarchy and social norms. The lines, the beauty, the pressure of perfection, and all of those things. And that is not what I sense from Graham. What I sense from her is the power of the individual, which is a very American thing—an individualistic society and giving freedom to the individual.

There are stereotypes [in Graham's repertory]. It's just that the woman gets the main role and gets to be subtle. You are part of a world where women have the possibility to have subtlety. It is a good thing, it's a really good thing. When you get to the core of it, you really see how political she was and how feminist she was and maybe the most political thing she did was not to call it political. You have to play the game of institutions. It's a very specific thing to start from the pelvis. It's something we should have knowledge about. To start deep in your body in a society where it is the brain, the brain. For a woman to have her body, just have her body. That is already a lot.[17]

Past to Present

All of the dancers, artists, and administrators whom I have interviewed throughout this book have impressed me with their passion for the life of the Graham canon and with their very personal interpretations of it. Each artist has employed the work of the canon to serve their own creative visions and have simultaneously supported and inspired the community at large. These actions in themselves are also part of the lineage where one person's action can spark another's.

Lloyd Knight, principal dancer with the Martha Graham Dance Company, is one of today's most vibrant personalities on the New York dance scene. He first studied Graham technique with former principal dancer Peter London and Fredric Frature in Miami, Florida. Lloyd's passion for Graham's movement and aesthetics is infectious. In this interview he speaks about this passion and his hopes for the future of the Company.

LK   *I started training in Graham technique at New World School of the Arts in Miami, Florida, and I had two teachers in the beginning Fredric Frature and Peter London. After a while, Peter London, who was a principal dancer with the Graham Company as well, he really became my mentor. I started doing summer and winter intensives at the Graham School up until graduation. Then I did the audition senior year with Terese [Capucilli] and Christine [Dakin] and I got in! So that kind of was it, I have been in the Company since 2005.*

---

[17] Personal interview with Rafael Molina.

FIGURE 17 *Lloyd Knight in a photograph by Gregory Vaughan.*

My place in the Graham Company, starting off it was only Graham work, which was really, really great. I always say it was like an intensive for me because they started me from the bottom and I worked my way up. But yeah it was just Graham work year after year, and it was really great. It was a great learning experience being around a lot dancers who had been there much longer than me, so they had that knowledge and all of these gems that I was surrounded by. Then we started doing contemporary work, newer pieces. In 2007 we started doing the Lamentation Variations. And that was kind of the start before Janet brought in full-on ballets. It *was a slow process for me (accepting contemporary), but also a process that I was pretty open to it as long as it was a choreographer that I respected and I felt like they respected us and our home, being in Graham's house. I've enjoyed it.*

BWM *With new choreographers, is there anything that you feel is a misunderstanding or misperceptions that you feel are important to you? What would you like for dancers, choreographers, and audiences to know about the Graham dance canon that you feel is currently missing in the general perception of this body of work?*

LK *In general people always think that we move in this very boxed type way. But I feel that is the total opposite of how a Graham dancer moves. I actually feel that we are the perfect mix of qualities of a dancer because we can be sharp, soft, we have that dramatic aspect too. But that is the number one thing that frustrates me—that people think we can only move in one way. And when they demonstrate that way, I am like, "I don't know who moves like that; nobody in the history has ever moved like that."*

But I think lately the people who don't know [the work] who go to see the Company, they are really surprised. Even if they don't see the contemporary work, if they go to an all-Graham night, they just get really surprised, like "I didn't know that Graham dancers could move like that." Even in her dances, yes, she has a codified technique, and you see different movements repeated but in different ways. Each of her ballets is completely different.

BWM *The technique came out of a physical female form (Martha Graham). Is there anything that has been an opening to you in terms or connected to that idea?*

LK *Yes. I think it is interesting. Let's say ballet, for example, I feel like you [male dancer] have your place. You're a male dancer, and you perform these duties, but I feel like there's not that much room for you to fully dive in and express yourself. Maybe that's wrong of me to say because I am not a professional ballet dancer. But in Graham, for me, there is no difference (between the sexes) when I am in Graham class. Yes, it is from a female perspective, a female body, but it is just dance to me. And I am just trying to accomplish these movements. But at the same time, I do feel like she has allowed me to really dive in and be comfortable with really being vulnerable to everybody and with myself. To just put that out there in the Graham work, in the technique, you have to incorporate all the mind, body, spirit as far as I am concerned. It's very freeing for me.*

BWM *Along with that, what comes up for you when I say the phrase "the House of the Pelvic Truth"?*

LK   *The sexual center* [laughing]. *It's your sexual center. Things are created from your pelvic truth* [laughing again] *from your sexual center. It's the connection that all the limbs attach to. For me, yes, the sexual center, the pelvic truth. That's something I have to keep thinking about. For her work, the contraction and release, everything starts from the pelvis. So without that, it's just not going to happen at all. That visceral gut everything takes place down there, life.*

In some of her pieces, the males are ultra-masculine, almost caveman-like. It's all fantasy and role playing, I enjoy it.

BWM   *What about being a place of affirmation or support? Where in the overculture there is a heteronormative default mode?*

LK   *I think it goes back to the physicality of her work and the technique. You just get drawn to it. That's what speaks to you. It supports me and my feelings of dancing. I am a gay male dancer, and it supports that, and I feel comfortable in it. I do feel like also in the Graham work there is a level of theater that at least for myself I can go crazy in and all the fantasies. I might not be performing the female part, but there is something about the theatrical part of it that really draws me in.*

I keep thinking about Graham compared to classical ballet. I feel like if I'm going to walk this way, why am I really walking this way, what does this movement mean? Everything means something emotionally; it comes from an emotional standpoint.

BWM   *What is it about Graham, why doesn't it die? The dancers keep reviving it. There are people who have tried to stamp it out, crush it, and it just keeps coming back and it comes back because the dancers bring it back. What is it?*

LK   *It's that work and she speaks the truth. I think out of every technique I have encountered, it is just the realness. And I say real, I mean, it really starts with you. Everybody is going to do turns around the back differently. But it comes from your center, from your pelvic truth, and everything grows on top of that. I think people can connect with that. You start on the floor and you grow yourself up* [laughing]. *The work is just very deep, very real. It is from a female point of view, but it is from a human point of view. We are not fairies or swans or anything like that; it is from a human regard. So, I think that's why people come back to it; it is real and it is raw. People come to see the Company, and people are gagged they just can't believe what they saw.*

Her Rite of Spring *for example. There is not that much to it movement wise. We repeat a lot of steps, but the way she constructed it and laid it out. Of course there is the music, but even if you take away the music, the rawness of the dancers and how they have to move throughout the space. Even in her lyrical softer work as well, the different aspects of love. Everybody can connect to love, and you are just humans in space being human.*

BWM   *What have you learned physically in doing the Graham technique? What kind of physical discoveries have you made?*

LK   *Probably most importantly is the use of the torso. Being able to really soften. Some people say, curve the back, curve the spine. Even if you just say "contract," but what does it really mean to contract making space in between separating, thinking about the space all around you? So if were are facing the front of the class and we are doing our exercises, but we are thinking about the people behind us as well. How does that look from that perspective? I think the most for me, the torso. I have learned a lot, and I still continue to learn a lot about the use of the upper body. I think for her work, it's most important.*

BWM   *Would you talk about a memorable role or a role that has been significant in understanding her philosophy of dance or being a dancer?*

LK   *I always talk about* Embattled Garden, *which was my first big taste of a role. Being onstage the whole time, you never get to leave the stage. I felt like I entered a world where everything was at its highest. We are performing on works of art, Isamu Noguchi sets, which are beautiful and these gorgeous costumes and all of the other performers around you onstage. For me, that was a big stepping stone because I had to number one be in the moment the whole time. So that was a really big deal for me. I learned along the way of course, even after performing it a couple of times. But to have the theory of the topic that was going on and portraying it in that way and have the information there in my mind to get out to the public and to have a dialogue with the other characters as well in that piece, for me* Embattled Garden *was it.*

BWM   *And who were your coaches on that? Or who did you watch on video, who were your references?*

LK   *Christophe* [Jeannot] *a lot. I watched Christophe a lot, he was awesome. And also Maurizio* [Nardi], *Maurizio for sure! And then there were archival films of Clive Thompson and … there are so many. And then in studio coaching, I had, Donlin* [Foreman] *even coached me once, which was awesome.*

BWM   *Isn't it something that you can have even one coaching session with someone and it can embed within your performance? Even just an hour with someone.*

LK   *Yes! Peter London, of course, he was there for my first show actually. It was really important for me, it really clicked. You know, you watch Graham growing up and you're like, "Yeah, I get it, that's cool, that's fierce," but until you are in it … There have been shows of* Embattled Garden, *and the curtain comes down, and I am like, "I don't even know what happened." You are so into it and keep spiraling up and up and up and up. I think that is the goal of every dancer's performance actually is to just fully lose yourself in what you are doing. The physicality, at least for* The Stranger, *is through the roof. From the beginning to the end. I mean, we start the piece hanging upside down!*

BWM   *What do you think the benefits of studying Graham's technique and her work in general could be for that dancer?*

LK   *Simply, it is a structure, a classic modern dance structure. I find that a lot of people kind of lack that. Yes, they can move in these new contemporary ways, which are awesome, but for them to just simply know their body in that way. It's a complex question because they know their bodies obviously. They are doing all of these ridiculous fantastic things, but just the simple structure of Graham technique and learning how to sit up straight. What does it mean to spiral against that and the truth of the pelvic floor and how you use your pelvis and what comes on top of that and what explodes from that, I think that's the most important. Also, the simple regard for the technique. The movement brings out the drama if you will.*

You know you go to rehearsals, you perform, you get off the stage or even when you are onstage, you have these moments when you're like, wow, look at what I'm doing, this gift! And I remember you telling me back in the day, you were saying, "Dance is a gift, dance has given us everything that we have." And dance has given me everything that I have right now you know. I started dancing with Graham right out of school, and sixteen years later dance has given me my life right now. I dance for Graham, so Graham has given me everything that I have. I appreciate it a lot, and I hope that the world appreciates her work as well.

It is beautiful and people connect to her work. And now we are doing all this online teaching and I think it's really great that in a class you have people taking Graham class from all around the world. It's wild.

For a lot of people, they see Graham and they see the truth. They are like dance classic modern—the lightbulb goes off, and they're like, "damn, what?" So, I think something is happening in dance right now where people are really acknowledging the significance of Martha Graham and what she brought to dance and the people that came from her and everything that evolved from her. So I think it's a good thing happening right now.

Lorenzo Pagano, another powerful and poetic dancer began working with the Company very early in his dance career. Currently a soloist dancing principal roles in both classical Graham repertory and new contemporary commissions, Lorenzo shares his story and hopes for the future of the Company.

LP *I come from Torino, Italy. I started dancing when I was eleven years old and attended a dance school called Arke. It is a private school, and their main focus is American modern dance, especially the techniques of Martha Graham, Doris Humphrey, and Lester Horton, and then of course ballet. I got hooked into the Graham world through classes that I started taking when I was eleven or twelve years old. First of all, I couldn't really understand, especially in Graham because it takes a little time, you need to be prepared mentally to receive that knowledge and not just physically. Physically you can be able to do it, but when you know the intention, when you know what the story is and the mind behind it, it becomes very different. For me that happened when Kim Jones was coming every summer to my school to give courses. I met her when I was around thirteen years old, and from then she was one of my mentors for dance. I saw her in 2006 in her dance* Deep Song, *and she then reconstructed* Steps in the Street *on the ensemble of my school. I was just mesmerized.*

Seeing Kim in Deep Song *was something very unusual and I really liked it. I liked the repertory more than the technique. So from that moment, I really wanted to do the repertory. I was really drawn to the repertory of Martha Graham more than the technique. After high school, I came to study for six weeks in New York. I did three weeks of Graham's winter intensive, Kim gave me a scholarship for that. I wanted to go to Ailey [the Alvin Ailey School] because I was taking class in Vienna [Austria] with Milton Meyers,*[18] *and he said that I should go to Ailey. I loved Horton— it was another technique that I really enjoyed, and we were doing Ailey repertory. So I came [to New York] for six weeks. I wanted to do three weeks Graham and three weeks at Ailey so that I could decide which school I wanted to go to. In my mind, I knew it was Ailey even if I knew that I loved Graham, but it was Ailey in my mind. But then I came and studied for three weeks of the intensive at Martha Graham taught by Steve Rooks, Peggy Lyman, and Lone Larson, and I was dancing* Rite of Spring *as repertory with Steve Rooks. So that changed a lot [for me].*

When you do Graham outside of the Graham Center, it's very different. The technique is taught very differently because it's so hard to get. Once I got into the Graham School and started to really get the knowledge inside of the movement, what is beyond the movement, what is beyond the body, what is beyond the dance that happens beyond those four walls— something just clicked. It changed so much my idea of what dance was and what Graham was and what I wanted my path to be.

---

[18] Legendary teacher of Horton technique.

I was getting stronger. I was nineteen at that time, and the body changes a lot at that age. But also that technique builds you from the inside out. It builds so much the body, the discipline is so hard, that I felt a change daily. Not just in the understanding of the exercises, the routine of exercise [such as] what was the leg opening, you open the right and then you close with the left arm and then you pitch forward. Not just the routine, but how do you lift? From where do you lift? How do you contract? From where do you contract?

BWM   *Where? Where is it? From where do you contract?*

LP   *From your pelvic floor. That I understood maybe four years ago, and I was into the Company already four years. It's so easy, especially in Graham, to get a video—you copy shapes. We are very well trained in that as dancers. Then when you start doing those same exercises over and over for months, then it becomes years, and then it becomes almost a decade, it changes. The body knows what it is doing, the muscles are ready to do it, but the last thing that changes is your mind.*

How do you approach, how do you come into class, how do you start class, how do you warm up for class? That is all a preparation for the ritual that you start the moment you step into class. You sit down and you start your exercise, and from there you build up a whole new dimension with your mind and you train your body. But mostly I feel like Graham is a mind training. It is a dance form, it is a dance technique, and I think it is so valid to strengthen the body. And I think dancers that have a solid preparation in Graham and in ballet become very strong. They can do a lot of things.

There is a false idea that Graham dancers are very stiff and that they are only capable of doing Graham. This is what I was told many times when I was choosing where I wanted to go. That comes from the false idea of copying shapes, but once you really understand … and it takes years. I feel like in today's world, we don't have enough patience to really dig and stick with something long enough to really get to that point. But when you get there and really understand the movement from the body and from the mind, you become very free. And when you do other pieces or other choreographies, other techniques, you use Graham. It doesn't mean that you change it into a Graham shape, but you use that vocabulary to get to the other movement.

For example, when we did Echo *from Adonis Foniodakis, that was my second year in the Company, and it was totally different. It was super fast, limbs needed to be thrown away, everything was almost like a splash— you moved your body like you throw bucket of water on the floor and it splashes. It's kind of that. I remember thinking, "OK, I need to use my Graham core because if this is strong, then I can move everything very*

*freely and fast because I have control." So from that discipline I have the
freedom to move in other ways. That is something that's very important
for Graham, and I think it's something that's misinterpreted in the world. I
think it needs to be changed.*

BWM   *Graham created these archetypal male roles. Do you feel that in
these roles you are still able to express and/or represent what you choose
or want to express?*

LP   *Yes, because there is always this idea of the Graham man in Graham
roles to be this muscular, big, very strong guy who moves just in two
dimensions and is there for the woman and that's it. Also, before I joined
the Company people were telling me you're very skinny for the Graham
Company. I had the idea that I am not big enough to do* Errand into the
Maze, *I'm not big enough to do* Cave of the Heart, *all of these roles. I
entered the Company with this concept like I need to be this, and this
is the man in this company, this is the role of the man. In a Graham
piece, usually there is an introduction, a development, and then there is
a realization that is the climax of the drama and then the end. And that
moment of the realization of what happened in the story is different for
every piece; that is the moment where everything drops for the man.*

   *All the power, the strength that he has also drops, and at the end he feels
almost empty and you are vulnerable. And that is something that nobody
ever told me. That's the side of the man in Graham that no one ever talks
about. Everyone focuses on how you need to do the lift, you need to be
strong, lift the woman, you need to be fierce, and you have to show off.
But nobody says but what happens then. And that is what draws me more
and more into Graham. The beginning is the decoration; when you get to
the center you get to the essence of it. It is not that machismo stuff of a
figure. It is the figure on the floor; she has killed your mother, they killed
your princess. In the end, it is pretty brutal in terms of emotion, it's very
draining. There is a lot of emotion that I feel, in the twentieth century, was
not shown. The figure of the man was not shown; a man crying, a man
being hurt, the man was always a strong figure. And I like that [about
Graham theater] because it's not true. Graham men are not strong all the
time. I was really drawn by it a lot.*

BWM   *Which roles have been significant to you so far in your career?*

LP   *There is so much! The good news is that in the course of her
life Graham had so many inspirations that you can be so much in her
repertory. I always have been drawn to mythology, maybe because I am
from Italy, so that's very close to me. I grew up with that civilization—the
Romans, which came from the Greeks. So* Night Journey *and* Cave of

the Heart *are two examples of what I was saying before about that male figure and the stereotype of the big, strong, male dancer. At the end, at the climax of the piece hits, and everything crumbles down, and also the idea of the male figure crumbles down. Doing those two pieces brought me to the full realization of what is the role of the man and Graham. I also enjoy so much the more abstract pieces where you can really invest yourself into your own world, into your own story.* Dark Meadow *is one of those,* Diversion of Angels—*it's not a prescribed story for not portraying a character, but it's more than that; you have the freedom in your mind to create your own story, to create your own environment and connection with the other dancers. I love abstract pieces for that reason.*

As dancers we always say you need to overcome your limitations. And I feel like in the Graham technique, I really went beyond my limitations in some aspects. For example, my lower back has always been very problematic, and every doctor said when you curve your lower back that is the worst thing you could do. And I curve my back all day every day! And just to be able to find my way of working through that technique with my body it is magical. It is the best thing you can discover because you discover your body, you know that limits, but you work every day more and more to get one inch more every day, whatever it is. Spine stretch or tilts or spiral, lifting the contraction, every day you work toward that goal and your body changes. Your body changes!

BWM   *How would you describe your current company? What do you think are the similarities and differences of the current company in 2020 and say the grand company ten or twenty years ago or any generation actually?*

LP   *Things have changed in the Graham Company where the focus is still in the Graham repertory, but not only. The focus is also on what's happening outside of the Graham world that can emphasize it, contradict it, stimulate this repertory and the dancers in so many possible ways. It's very refreshing to have new choreographers. It's not a good match with everybody of course, and that's OK, you learn from everything. But it's very challenging, it's very pleasant to have this difference, almost like a different dress that you wear every single hour of rehearsal. It's disorienting but it can become familiar.*

Honestly, there's nothing like Graham. You start working with a choreographer, and you might like it or you might not like it. It might be good for your body, or it may cause a lot of injury to your body, you never know. More and more you absorb that way of dancing, and it is great because you acquire more and more knowledge that you can bring back to Graham—the physical information. This feeds Graham also, which is great. That does not mean to get out of the Graham but it keeps you on your toes, it keeps you alive. Not having the founder anymore makes it hard to find the way in Graham. What is the way?

Graham has a lot of tastes, points of view from a lot of people. Most of the time one is black and one is white, and you're like, "What am I going to choose?" So you make your own choices, and the more that you are familiar with the work, the more you feel comfortable doing it. And I feel like back in the day, maybe her voice was fresher. She just passed away or it was very few years since she passed away, but I think her words and her energy were still there. While today we have people who have worked with her, and they are doing a great job in many ways carrying on the legacy, but twenty-eight years have passed [since her death]. Luckily we have a lot of written documents, a large archive where you can go look for information, for interviews, you can still see that on the video, but I think that time is a big factor.

I just feel Graham is so complete. It's not just the technique, it's not just a dance. It's that every single aspect is taken care of, whether it is lighting, music, costumes, settings, make-up, placement onstage, movement of course, relationships, head pieces, props, capes. Everything has a purpose and is there for a reason, and I feel that in today's dance world that craft is lost.

BWM   *What do you think is the benefit of a young dancer who is in training studying Graham technique outside of the Graham School, for example in a conservatory in Italy? What would be the benefit, if there is one in your opinion?*

LP   *When I grew up, I was always told, "You have to study ballet because ballet is the base of dance," and you will really build up your body with that. I think Graham is the base, one of the bases of contemporary dance. A lot of what we call today contemporary dance comes from that world. The curve and the extension of the torso. If you go to see Batsheva, you see this movement like a big fourth position in grand pile and giant curves very different. They curve in and out but do not arrive to her release; it goes beyond the release of arching the other way, so it's like a display of the concave and the convex curves. It's a display that all comes from Graham. It's a use of the torso that I see a lot in Batsheva, in Alvin Ailey. There are many contemporary art forms which use the spiral, how you turn using the back and not just your head. I find it in so many contemporary styles.*

So I feel like Graham, and it's not the only one, there are so many modern dance techniques. Graham helped develop Cunningham, and Cunningham help developed another branch of the dance world, like Richard Alston and Pam Tanowitz now. Graham is one of the seeds of contemporary dance, and it's important that even if you don't like the seeds but you like the tree. Even if you don't like it, you need to respect it—that is very important. I think it is a valid technique to build your body in a very different way than ballet, but I think both techniques combined make a very good training. I think it's very relevant today, even if you really don't like the repertory, it gives you something—it gives to a totally different perspective on how to use the idea of the fall, the idea of knee work, how to lift yourself while you're doing knee work. All contemporary forms are using the knees, and it is relevant to know where that comes from in contemporary dance. Partnering, when you really understand how to get on top of your sit bones and lift yourself up from your core and elongate the spine, then when you get lifted you have the same principle, and you become so light that your partner will really appreciate it. The release in breathing, if you use that energy it is going to help you so much.

I hope it will keep flourishing and keep that work alive. Maybe it's because I come from a culture where preservation is the number one thing. In Italy, it is like the Coliseum and St. Pietro, the church. Even in my hometown, my mom lives in a house from the 1500s. So for me preservation has always been very important. To come to America and be part of one of the oldest groups that have been created in this country is very special. I think it's important because you cannot deny the origin of anything; without the origin you would not be there. So you need to respect every historical dance form, no matter what. It's great because there is still a group of dancers who are drawn to it, and once you get into that spiral it's hard to get out!

Currently Artistic Associate and Rehearsal Director for the Company, Denise Vale was a principal dancer during the 1980s and 1990s. She is responsible for maintaining both classical and contemporary dances within the repertoire. Known for her strength and passion, in this interview she shares some of her significant thoughts on the lineage.

DV   *I found Martha by chance. A group of us young dancer humans let loose on the world questioning the purpose of life watched the PBS film of Clytemnestra in a rundown squatters apartment in West Philly.[19] We had no expectations, but then there it was,* Clytemnestra … *the sheer beauty of the technique, modern architecture of the bodies' physical shapes, the astounding virtuosity, and then I was stunned by the humanity of her characters and the journey into the human psyche that her work insisted, demanded I see! It was a life-changing afternoon, though there would be more years still roaming the city questioning life and dance. Bertram Ross was my first Graham class and Graham teacher at Ailey,[20] and I crawled out of his class exalted and physically exhausted. My body that day found out it loved the Graham technique. That is my lineage to*

---

[19] Philadelphia, Pennsylvania.
[20] The Ailey School.

Graham, all else after was the day-to-day struggle to be hired as a Graham dancer. However, when I was sixteen, I had given my Dad a reel-to-reel of Appalachian Spring *for his birthday. He never listened to it, but I fell in love and danced in the living room to it over and over again, never knowing it was the musical score created for Martha. Fate? I loved all of my teachers; if I name one, I will have to name everyone. A nugget of truth from each wonderful instructor whether I wanted to hear it or not. I always loved my corrections. The absolutely delightful experience of learning through dance, loved it!*

Martha's brownstone on 63rd street, a house that housed the fabulous Graham Company and School. The Company worked in the main studio on the first floor. There was a garden off of the east side of the studio, warm wooden floors, Noguchi benches lined the front, sets and props lined the sides ready for a full day's rehearsal. The terror of it all, the beauty of it all, the presence of Martha in the room, waiting for her to arrive in her limo. The door opens to studio one and here she is. I am at a heightened level of living suddenly and I realize I am not alone in this feeling as I look around.

I was told by an original dancer at Graham who came to visit that I looked nothing like a Graham dancer, she even took me outside the studio to tell me. I actually thought she would say something nice, but not these strong, fabulously real Graham ladies, and so my challenges started almost immediately. First prove her wrong, but then, more importantly and for my dancer soul I was trying to nurture ... find the damn artist hiding in me. I was given the role of The Maid in Seraphic Dialogue. *I worked on this one small passage of when Joan of Arc hears voices and thought, "How can I be honest in my hearing?" and I did it over and over and over again because I was always thinking not good, go back again, you don't mean it, everyone will know! We were in Oslo, Martha came in to observe, she says at the end of the dance, well some of you are honest and some of you are not and all I could say was I hope I was honest ... that was the challenge of every ballet I performed from there on after.*

BWM   *Which roles have been significant to you in your career?*

DV   *The Chorus in* Cave of the Heart, Lamentation, Serenata Morisca, *The Attendant in* Herodiade, *Clytemnestra in* Clytemnestra.

BWM   *What are one or two of the Graham philosophies that are meaningful/inspiring to you in your work with the Company?*

DV   *Philosophically speaking, to be honest in the interpretation of a role given, consistent in execution, to find my own inner voice so that the choices I make in rehearsal and onstage arise from my unique interpretation of her work.*

BWM   *How do you experience the technique as a significant force for releasing/honoring/exploring the female form or the female body?*

DV   *I find it more interesting to explore the universal psychology of the human experience through my singular female brain. Dancing from the pelvic center is an experience natural to man and animals alike, birthing and hunting for instance. The anatomical positioning of the vital organs residing in the torso, not the limbs, or a toenail allows me to utilize the power of nature. In the act of honoring nature, I experience my female form as well as the less dominant characteristics of my male tendencies. I love them both.*

BWM   *What would you like for dancers, educators, and audiences to know about the Graham dance canon that you feel is currently missing in the general perception of this body of work?*

DV   *Is something missing? Stay true to the body of work known as the Martha Graham technique! It will reveal all regarding nature and the human condition. Avoid entirely the politicization of her work or you will miss the beauty of her original intention, to explore the inner landscape of the human heart.*

BWM   *When did you become Rehearsal Director/Artistic Associate, and what qualities do you look for in dancers joining the Company today?*

DV   *I joined in 2007. I look for some level of expertise in the Graham technique, and if possible an innate sense of dramatic feeling for her choreographic content. A dancer willing to serve Graham first and foremost.*

BWM   *What are some of your hopes or aspirations for the work and the lineage?*

DV   *I hope that we do not lose the intensity of the Graham technique, that we stay true to that which gave it its reason to exist and thrive. To honor the generations of dancers, musicians, sculptors, singers, poets, and confidants who have all, through a great passion and love, contributed to Martha's body of work. To avoid and resist the temptation to water down the great humanity of her work through the superficial lens of the momentary politics of the day. To paraphrase Abraham Lincoln, "Laws change, people die, the land remains."*

In the final interview of this book we learn from former principal Graham dancer Virginie Mécène, currently Director of Program and Director of Graham 2 for the Martha Graham School. Virginie speaks about her experience and responsibility with in the lineage.

VM   *I joined the Martha Graham Dance Company in 1994 and was among the first generation of dancers "post-Martha"; she died in 1991. At the time, there was a nucleus of dancers who would not leave the Company while Martha was alive, and they stayed on for a few years after that. So when I joined the Company, most of the other Company members were already there for a long time. They had worked with Martha Graham herself Terese Capucilli, Christine Dakin, Donlin Foreman, Denise Vale, Joyce Herring, Pascal Rioult, Thea Barnes, Maxine Sherman … Janet Eilber had already left the Company for a few years, but she came back as a guest. All these beautiful dancers, whom I had seen onstage while I was at the school, were very inspiring. They all had worked very closely with Martha in the process of creating new dances and interpreting others. It was just impressive, very intimidating in a way to be in the Company among them all. Each of them had their own beautiful, wild, and extended personalities—bigger than themselves because that is what the work wants you to do. That is what Martha was trying to get her dancers to do, to be themselves ten times over. It felt as if you were literally on sacred ground. The School at the time was on 63rd Street, between first and Second Avenue. It was an old townhouse building with a garden on each side. Studio 1, where we were rehearsing at the time, and the other two studios had a wood floor. I kept wondering how many dancers had "sweated" on these floors over the years. It must have been hundreds, including many greats. It was a sacred place. When the building was destroyed, I kept a piece of that floor.*

BWM   *What made that floor so special?*

VM   *Wood reacts to the heat and the humidity. So, it would react to our bodies. It would react to our body heat, sweat, and blood I guess. We were not using air conditioning, except when Martha was around, so we would be dancing in the heat of the summer and that floor would react a lot. It could be very sticky or slippery or it could be just perfect for you. That floor was "alive." There was a whole relationship with the floor because, as you know, the Graham technique is very grounded. I remember the warmth of the wood like it is a part of you, and even now as you ask these questions, I remember the sensation while touching the wood with the side of my hands for the falls. I still feel the wood of that studio on my body. There were also those beautiful low wooden benches [in the studio], I believe they were Noguchi pieces. At that time, we just took it for granted to sit on those beautiful pieces of art; we would just sit there casually. Looking back, realizing what we were around, it was quite extraordinary.*

BWM   *What was the Company dynamic at that time? Were the new dancers accepted by the ones who had worked with Graham? Did you feel friction?*

VM   *I think it was separate and integrated at the same time. People had their histories there and their experiences that you could not catch up with; you had to go through your own. At the same time, dancing among them, feeling them, sweating with them was a way to step up and be transported into a different world, a different level of understanding things. The first season I performed with the Company was at Brooklyn Academy of Music, and I was in seven ballets. One of them was Heretic and I remember the energy of Denise Vale particularly because she had the amplitude of a beautiful and powerful eagle. I remember her commenting on shifting. In one of the moves I had to change the choreographic formation from a curve to a line, and I only had three steps to do so. There was no way the rest of the cast would accommodate the new dancers; the new ones just had to step up right away and I remember doing just that. That energy from these dancers would push you to deliver immediately.*

Dancers had their ways of passing on all of those needs for moving bigger than yourself, such as shifting, delivering everything in the now, to push yourself. It was part of the philosophy of being there. [The dancers] were amazing examples. About Terese and Christine, I remember wondering, "What is the secret that Martha told them? For them to dance like that, she must have told them a secret—what is it?" And then I realized that the secret was perseverance, hard work, accepting to empty yourself, to reveal yourself as if being naked, and explore, dig, rebuild, pushing through, and discovering who you are through this artwork. I became a part of it, even if Martha wasn't there. I think that those dancers took it upon themselves to protect the work and tried to deliver it as best they could with the memories of Martha. It wasn't uncommon to hear these phrases, "No, it is not that way, it is this way" or "Martha wanted it this way." In a way, it was like hearing Martha herself because it was freshly passed on from their experience of working with her. When I was a student at the School, Martha Graham was alive, so I got chances to have her in class, not teaching herself but observing while somebody else was teaching, and she would gather us around her and give corrections to everyone in the class. Most of her corrections were about breathing. It was all about the breath. That is what I remember the most about her comments, the breath.

When I came to the Graham School in 1988, being in America, being in New York, and seeing all of these dance figures still alive; it was like walking into my dance history book. Martha Graham was there, Merce Cunningham was there and still performing, Erick Hawkins and others were still creating. So there were all those people around, and it was amazing. Also, my teachers at the Graham School were many illustrious artists who danced with Martha in the 1940s and 1950s: Ethel Winter, Ethel Butler, Pearl Lang, Sophie Maslow, Yuriko, Mary Hinkson, and Linda Hodes. Although Jane Dudley, Bob Cohan, and David Wood were not teaching regularly at the time, they occasionally gave either workshops, lectures, or sometimes coached when we worked on a dance they were in. I remember taking a class with Bertram Ross at Mary Anthony's studio. They would come to visit and talk to us. It was like a big family.

It was also a time when reconstructions of major works, such as Panorama by Yuriko (1992) and "Prelude to Action," from Chronicle *(1994), by Sophie Maslow, were being made. I was one of the dancers in the process for these two reconstructions. Although both Yuriko and Sophie had different ways of working, it was a very enriching experience to be participating in the deciphering of the materials from early 1920s footages, and translating them into a more "evolved" technique.*

I had also other generations of teachers from the 1960s, 1970s, the 1980s: Diane Gray, Carol Fried, Peggy Lyman, Takako Asakawa, Bert Terborgh, Kevin Keenan, Amgard von Bardeleben, Jacqulyn Buglisi, and Donlin Foreman. There were also some Company members teaching, such as Denise Vale and Kenneth Topping. Right there you had different generations of dancers: those from the 1940s and 1950s and then those from the late 1960s, 1970s, and 1980s. You could see how it was passed on through them and their respect and admiration they had for the other generations. It was a beautiful place to be in, filled with knowledgeable people, with a lot of quality and passion. You could feel that these people had spent their lives around Graham. Martha Graham herself but also the Graham world that they made for themselves, it was very rich. So receiving a correction on your breathing from Martha Graham made a lot of sense, as it was always emphasized with other teachers. Having her saying it and demonstrating it (she was already late in her nineties and she could still open up her chest) was a memorable experience. When she passed by you in the School, she would stop and say "Hello." She had very strong energy; even though she was petite and frail, you could see her strength through her eyes and feel her strong personality. When she looked at you with her piercing eyes, it felt like she could see everything inside of you. This world becomes part of the people who go through it and they give their own [part] as well. You absorb the energy of everybody, and it becomes your energy in a way. The dancers were very faithful to Martha in trying to preserve the work in the ways that they had experienced it. They were passing it on, and they would not accept it to be done any other way. Over the years, that changed a little bit.

BWM *How did that feel, the restriction upon you?*

VM   *I did not feel it as a restriction because I felt that I had so much to learn; it opened up a new world instead. We were like sponges. Years later I learned to make my own choices based on the different inputs I was receiving from different coaches. Being coached by dancers of different generations opened up different views. Interestingly, the older generations were more open to letting you make choices for yourself. Perhaps because they had more time to remove themselves and had more experience at nurturing artists. Or perhaps because in their time, they had more choices themselves, being part of the formative years of the Company. I danced in the Company for twelve years and went through all the ranks from Apprentice to Principal. I worked under several directors Carol Fried with Ron Protas, Terese Capucilli with Christine Dakin, and Janet Eilber. As the years went by, the Company had its ups and downs, and many dancers left and some new ones came in, but what is exceptional about this Company is the strong devotion that dancers have toward the work. There is a certain traditional way of approaching the work that is passed on from dancers to dancers, and that is strong and beautiful.*

BWM   *Was there a particular role in the repertory that you felt pushed you to be ten times yourself?*

VM   *All the roles require being ten times yourself, but* Deep Song *for example is one where I felt I had to go deeply into something that I wanted to express from inside myself without knowing exactly what it was. Digging and excavating the emotion is not always easy to do because the more you bring yourself out, the more you feel exposed and vulnerable. But if you ride along with this vulnerability, the journey becomes incredibly transporting, sharpening all your senses, and bringing the awareness of the instant. You are suddenly expressing yourself in a dimension that nothing can interrupt. You are simply being you, intensified.*

BWM   *Through your career, you became Director of the Graham School as well as Graham 2, the pre-professional company, which must have been a huge challenge and transition. What is your current role with the Graham organization?*

VM   *When I left the Company in 2006, I thought about doing something different and becoming a Pilates teacher. But it was a time when the Graham Center needed a director for the School and also for Graham 2 (called the Martha Graham Ensemble at the time). Ellen Graff and Marnie Thomas Wood were retiring from these positions, and I succeed them in January 2007. The first semester I started with my husband, Kevin Predmore,*[21] *as we both were hired for one semester as interim directors.*

---

[21] Kevin Predmore is a former Graham dancer, founding member of Buglisi/Foreman Dance, and a teacher of Graham technique at The Ailey School.

After the first semester, I stayed on alone as Director of the School (this title changed to Director of Program in 2015) as well as Artistic Director of Graham 2, to the present. I was aware through my experiences with the School, working with all of these different generations of Graham artists, and my twelve years of experience as a performer with the Company, that I had plenty to share. I did not want that to go to waste; it was a very natural, logical transition. Through the students, I felt like I was still dancing, still performing because I was sharing so much of my experience.

It was not easy to suddenly be directing a school and a performing troupe at the same time. There were many aspects I was discovering on the spot. Coordinating and hiring teachers, musicians, developing and creating new programs, creating syllabus, auditioning dancers, coaching, directing, programming, coordinating with technicians, and doing many sorts of administrative duties ... I used all of my instincts to understand what students needed while growing enrollments and operating within a very tight budget. I had to be very creative and resourceful.

Being a former international student myself—and the School has a lot of international students—I know that students come to achieve their dream, which for most is to be in the Company. I also know that it is not going to be possible for everybody. But it might be for some. It takes a lot of perseverance and work and belief to do it. I felt confident that I could guide them through, no matter what the outcome. Directing Graham 2 was a fantastic opportunity for me to pass on the Graham dances, the experiences of being in the studio with the dancers, the rehearsal process, giving them the tools to develop. Sharing all of those little performing details that come with experience, but also being able to step back and letting enough room for them to discover for themselves. I learned so much from coaching, directing, and programming the Graham work. In 2015 my title of Director of the School changed to Director of Program, which released me from the big administrative responsibilities. It suddenly opened more room for me to be more creative and I started to choreograph again.

Having completed the circle and coming back there as the Director of the School was an incredible honor. Altogether, I spent years at that School. From 1988 to the present, uninterrupted, except when I was in the Company, but even then I was teaching at the School, except during the suspended activities of the School and Company in 2000. Diane Gray was the Director of the School at the time I joined. I completely admire her. First of all, as a performer (I learned to know her as a performer through video), her personality, her way of directing the School, caring for all the students, and her elegance, were so inspiring. She did inspire me all of those years when I was a student, and suddenly I was in her director's shoes. I realized that this was a huge responsibility and that we were completely affecting student's futures step by step.

*Students create their futures, but they put their trust into our hands
to provide them the training they need to achieve their goals, and I feel
strongly that we have to give them the best we can. It is a big decision for
the parents to let their son or daughter come to New York City. For some
families, providing support for studies and living expenses takes a lot of
financial hardship as well. It is a big deal for families, and it is not to be
taken lightly. Having been in this situation myself, I wanted to make sure
our students would come through. Whether or not they will make it into
the Company, that is a different story. We provide them with vigorous
training and help them understand how to evolve and how to become a
professional dancer or teacher.*

*When possible, I travel abroad to give workshops and, many times,
I recruit students. Graham Company soloist, Charlotte Landreau, is an
example of many. She came to take a workshop/audition that I gave in
Paris. It must have been around 2013, and she was a very young girl who
came in from the Béjart School, in Lausanne, and she had some notions
of Graham but she still had a way to go. She was a gymnast when she
was younger, and she had the habit of sticking her ribs out as gymnasts
do when they salute. But, she had this great energy and had talent.
Over the week-long workshop, she was taking corrections well and had
perseverance, and at the end of the week, I sat her down at a café there and
said: "I would like to offer you a position in Graham 2 and a scholarship
to enroll in the professional training program," and it changed her life right
there. She had trained at the School and through Graham 2 for two years
and then got into the Company where she is doing very well, and she is
becoming a teacher as well. It is so great to see the evolution. So, I think
our decisions are very important. In our responsibilities as teachers and
directors, we help them shape their futures. It does change people's lives.*

BWM   *You have students who have gone through the program and gone
on to other companies (not only the Graham Company) and been very
successful as well.*

VM   *Yes, as a matter of fact, a lot of them went to the Graham Company,
but also Limón, Paul Taylor, Buglisi Dance Theater, Rioult Dance, Nai-Ni
Chen, Battery Dance, Michael Mao, and other prominent companies in
the US and Europe. When I attend a Graham Company or other concerts
where former students are shining on stage and living their dreams, it
is very rewarding. Former students also went on to become directors,
choreographers, and teachers and are sending us their students.*

*Besides the future of the students, I also felt that the future of the
instruction of the Graham technique was important. So, I compiled
a syllabus of the technique that is followed throughout the School
curriculum, and for over fifteen years I have been developing and leading
the pedagogy program, assuring a teaching training that meets the needs*

of today's dance world while maintaining the Graham fundamentals so that pedagogy students are ready to teach in whichever country they go back to upon graduation. I also created and developed a teacher workshop for teachers from over the world to learn about the technique and include some of its principles in their class.

BWM   *You have always been a choreographer. Do you feel that your work in Graham has affected your own artistic work?*

VM   *Absolutely. I choreographed before I came to New York but it was very light. Graham affected my way of looking at a piece and my way of digging and finding movement. The quote from Martha Graham, "It is not your business to determine how good it is, not how it compares with other expressions. It is your business to keep it yours clearly and directly, to keep the channel open," struck me specifically when I recreated* Ekstasis *because I just had a few pictures but I did not have a choreography. There was no film, so I did not know what the original choreography was, I just had too few pictures. I remember at some point thinking that, "I have no idea where this is taking me." I did not know what I was doing, but I had to create my starting point.*

    The original dance was created in 1933, and there were only a few lines from Martha Graham saying that she was experimenting with the pelvis and shoulder. I concluded that this must have been the starting point of her discovering her whole technique because she was experimenting with the pelvis. She did not say that for a fact, but I imagined that this could have been it. And so, it became my starting point. Perhaps, I have gone through the same process to create Ekstasis *that Martha may have gone through herself when creating her original version. Starting from a place deep within, digging in our ancestral memories, and finding a deep source of energy from which we can speak. So, digging for movements was not trying to "take" moves that she had created for another dance. My process was to go through my own exploration and excavate these movements from myself to make a dance. I learned to not be afraid of what is coming out of myself, no matter what people are going to say; it doesn't matter. Having doubts in the middle of the process is normal, but continuing and seeing what comes out, without thinking about it, and without judging it before it exists, is exposing what you are going to work with. So, that process of exploring from within, as understood through the Graham work, allows me to understand a way to work for myself.*

BWM   *It is kind of like, the technique teaches you how to do the dances and this process teaches you something about creating. You are being yourself in the process through that lens.*

VM   *Martha created something universal that speaks beyond her choreographic work. She found a path to connect the movement from an emotional place. When this is understood on a deep level, it takes you on a journey of self-exploration and self-discovery. It is that philosophy of being you ten times over, from inside out.*

BWM *Great metaphor! What are your hopes for the future of this legacy and canon, the art?*

VM *I hope the legacy continues to reach as many people as possible through detailed and thorough teaching, with an internal approach, and with special attention to the organic aspect of the technique over complex and dramatic movement phrases that are often tough prematurely to young dancers, thus, skipping the real fundamentals of the technique. There is more to it. This is what I have been focusing on through the pedagogic courses I develop over the years. When approached from the inside, Graham roots you and provides a channel to discover something deeper about yourself, but one must take the time to explore and not be afraid of taking the time and getting deeper. The language of the technique is fascinating, and one must learn and practice each step that builds strength and muscle memory and understand how they connect to another. It becomes so much richer this way.*

Martha used to say, there is no short cut to art, and I completely agree with that. It is all about the process. One must practice diligently to build his or her unique experience. That's what will bring depth to the artist dancer, and therefore touch the audience directly to their core. This is so fundamental and universal, so primal—we cannot lose the primal. For it is what connects us as humans.

Next Steps

I suppose it never ends, it just continues.

—Martha Graham[22]

How does any person individuate, develop their singularity, and fully realize their inherent creative potential? For Martha Graham it was through engaging dance in an extraordinary life filled with curiosity, collaborative discovery, and extreme rigor. Graham was a women of her time who took up the mantel of independence from societal norms and completely subsumed her identity into her work. Breaking from the puritanical ideals and values of her childhood, she activated her body-mind to create art through movement. Her mix of imagery, rhythms, design, and emotional content mined world cultures yet are expressed through the lens of her experience.

Nothing is completely original; everything has its source in something other than itself. That is the very nature of life. Graham explored her limits,

---

[22] A re-phrasing of T. S. Eliot's "In my end is my beginning."

FIGURE 18 *Illustration by Michael Authur. The Company during a period of artistic renewal.*

her personal inner landscape, and brought her imagination to life onstage in and the studio. She carved a path in the world, a space for other people to gain power, strength, and control through discovering our bodies *as a world*. As previously stated in its Introduction, this book serves to affirm the choices, creativity, and productivity of generations of people who walked into Martha's house to learn how to be a dance artist; how to carve out their own lives as artists in the face of all obstacles.

Dance is its own embodied epistemology. Its physical practice sensitizes us to feel what another feels. Dance primes us for compassion and empathy toward our fellow humans. Martha Graham's technique and repertory live through dancers as choreographic interventions in a culture of disembodiment. Twenty-first-century Western ideas have spilled out from the twentieth carrying a culture of disembodiment in its wake. This disconnect has been exacerbated and deepened by the necessary isolation of the global pandemic of 2020–1. For many people the profound disconnection from our very own physical lives generates poor physical and mental health. Apathy and segregation caused by a focus on perceived productivity drains both our mental and emotional bodies. Here is where dance comes in. Thriving dance traditions can provide a remedy to cultural dis-ease[23] through necessary participation in and care for the physical body and its environment.

---

[23] Inspiration from Louise Hay.

Why must Graham continue? People need to go back to cultural stories, narratives, and practices. We need to re-interpret, re-examine, and re-imagine the hidden meanings behind our accepted symbols[24] and to re-evaluate which stories we want to keep and which need to be released to time. Graham's canon is a vehicle for examining symbolic human action, this is why it must continue to be performed. Those dancers who constitute the Martha Graham Dance Company are, at any given time, the highest level of the canon's articulation, embodiment, and realization. It is primarily through the physical practice of her technique that the dancer and audience access her vision; a vision that was initially synthesized through a female body in the twentieth century. Graham perceived life through her physicality and translated her perceptions into dances for her contemporary world. This primal, elemental, essential connection to the natural dancing body holds the potential to strip away the artifice of colonized civilization and reveal, through intensely personal effort, the universal One.

And ...

---

[24] Paraphrasing Carl Jung.

Postscript: Social Distancing, Dancing Online, #alonetogether

In 2020–1 a global pandemic killed millions of people around our world. Covid-19 stopped life as we knew it and changed the way that dancers and audiences experienced live performance. In a life-affirming phenomenon of action, people began dancing in videos and sharing them over social media platforms. Once again, Graham dancers were out front taking the lead, sharing their passion for Graham's technique and esthetic and inspiring thousands of artists and audiences from inside of their tiny apartments in New York City and around the world.

About the Photographers

Photographers and dancers share a symbiotic relationship, one feeds the other. Martha Graham and Barbara Morgan were iconic collaborators whose work together spawned the book *Martha Graham Sixteen Dances In Photographs*. Their work continues to inspire generations of photographers through the starkness and raw emotion captured in their collaboration. Through their rigor they created images together which would become lasting and emblematic of the period in which they worked. Twenty-first century photographers continue to be drawn to Graham's body of work for inspiration.

The photographers whose work have I selected to include in this book each have a particular purview and lens from which they view the canon. Paul B. Goode has photographed the Graham Company since 1984 when he first shot a rehearsal of her *Rite of Spring* at the Metropolitan Opera House in New York City. Since that time, Goode has returned to the work as a wellspring of reference and artistic collaboration. Christopher Jones came to photograph the Company after meeting company dancers in a photography workshop at Jacob's Pillow Dance Festival in Massachusetts, USA. He has focused on the dancers of the Company for ten years since that first encounter and developed his style of portraiture using the dancers' physicality and beauty. Brazilian photographer Guilherme Licurgo followed the Martha Graham Dance Company on tour to Italy and Greece from 2011–14 studying the dances, the dancers, and Graham's use of fabric. His creative adventure culminated in a beautiful art book, titled *Desert Flower*. Ken Browar and Deborah Ory (NYC Dance Project), whose image graces the cover of this book, have collaborated with dancers from the Graham Company by blending physicality and fashion in their book *Fashion & Dance: The Style of Movement*. Nan Melville has created an entire body of work photographing dance and dancers in New York City's vital dance scene over decades. I am grateful to all of these artists for sharing their work with me and allowing me to share it here.

INTERVIEWS

Elizabeth Auclair, December 27, 2020

Jacqulyn Buglisi, January 13, 2020

Terese Capucilli, May 13, 2020

Katherine Crockett, September 26, 2019

Christine Dakin, January 15, 2020

Javier Dzul, January 15, 2021

Janet Eilber, June 4, 2020

Donlin Foreman, August 26, 2020

Lloyd Knight, April 22, 2020

Lina Maria Gaviria Hurtado, August 22, 2020

Kim Jones, January 14, 2021

Virginie Mécène, July 16, 2020

Rafael Molina, January 1, 2021

Miki Orihara, August 17, 2020

Lorenzo Pagano, September 14, 2019

Abdiel Jacobsen, December 15, 2020

Denise Vale, September 16, 2021

Leslie Andrea Williams, June 26, 2020

SELECT BIBLIOGRAPHY

A Dancer's World [Film]. 1957. Peter Glushanok, Nathan Kroll, Martha Graham, and LeRoy Leatherman. WQED, released by Rembrandt Films.

Armitage, Merle. 1937. *Martha Graham*. Los Angeles: Lynton R. Kistler.

Arthur, Michael. 2003. *Return to Eden: The Rehearsal Drawings of Michael Arthur*. Self-published.

Berry, Wendell. 2012. *It All Turns on Affection: The Jefferson Lecture & Other Essays*. Berkeley, CA: Counterpoint.

De Mille, Agnes. 1991. *Martha: The Life and Work of Martha Graham*. New York: Random House.

Foreman, Donlin, Jacques D'Amboise, Marinella Guatterini, and Elisa Rondoni. 1992. *Out of Martha's House*. Rimini, Italy: Guaraldi Nuova Compagnia Editrice.

Gardner, Howard. 1994. *Creating Minds: An Anatomy of Creativity Seen through the Lives of Freud, Einstein, Picasso, Stravinsky, Eliot, Graham and Ghandi*. New York: Basic Books.

Graff, Ellen. 1997. *Stepping Left: Dance and Politics in New York City, 1928–1942*. Durham, NC: Duke University Press.

Graham, Martha. 1991. *Blood Memory*. New York: Washington Square

Graham, Martha. 2010. "I Am a Dancer." In *The Routledge Dance Studies Reader*. Ed. Alexandra Carter and Janet O'Shea, 95–100. London: Routledge.

Horosko, Marian. 1991. *Martha Graham: The Evolution of Her Dance Theory and Training, 1926–1991*. Chicago, IL: Chicago Review Press.

Horosko, Marian. 1991. "Martha's Prince: An Interview with Marian Horosko." *Dance Magazine*, Special Issue: Martha Graham (July).

Jones, Kim. 2015. "American Modernism: Reimagining Martha Graham's Lost Imperial Gesture (1935)." *Dance Research Journal*, 47 (3): 51–69.

Jung, C. G. 1948. "The Phenomenology of the Spirit in Fairy Tales." In *Collected Works of C.G. Jung*, vol. 9.1, *Archetypes of the Collective Unconscious*, 2nd ed., 207–54. Princeton, NJ: Princeton University Press.

Jung, C. G. 1953. *Collected Works of C.G. Jung*, vol. 12, *Psychology and Alchemy*.

Jung, C. G. 1968. "000226 Archetypes of the Collective Unconscious." In *Collected Works of C.G. Jung*, vol. 9.1, 2nd ed., 3–41. Princeton, NJ: Princeton University Press.

Lorde, Audre. 1982. *Uses of the Erotic: The Erotic as Power*. New York: Out & Out Books.

Martha Graham Dance Company. 1963. Interview with Walter Terry. Available online: https://www.92y.org/archives/martha-graham-walter-terry-essential-principles-dance (accessed July 19, 2021).

Martha Graham: Dance on Film[DVD]. 2007. Martha Graham Dance Company. Martha Graham, Peter Glushanok, Alexander Hammid, and LeRoy Leatherman. Irvington, NY: Criterion Collection.

Martha Graham Dance Company. 2020. Available online: https://marthagraham. org/history/ (accessed April 1, 2021).

Mills, Dana. 2017. *Dance and Politics: Moving beyond Boundaries*. Manchester: Manchester University Press.

Noguchi, Isamu. 1994. "Tribute to Martha Graham." *Isamu Noguchi: Essays and Conversations*. Ed. Diane Apostolos-Cappadona. New York: Harry N. Abrams, Inc.

Ockman, Carol. 2018. "PARAMODERNITIES #2 Female Trauma, Interdiction, and Agency in 'The House of Pelvic Truth. A Response to Martha Graham's Night Journey (1947).'" Avaibale online: https://performancepractice.org/ portfolio/paramodernities/ (accessed August 23, 2021).

Phillips, Victoria. 2020. *Martha Graham's Cold War: The Dance of American Diplomacy*. New York: Oxford University Press.

Radical Graham. 1994. By the Martha Graham Dance Company. Directed by Ronald Protas and Diane Gray. Brooklyn Academy of Music, Brooklyn, NY, September 28–October 9.

"Selections from the Martha Graham Collection." 2015. Library of Congress. Available online: http://lcweb2.loc.gov/diglib/ihas/html/marthagraham/ marthagraham-home.html (accessed July 1, 2020).

Shea, Murphy J. 2007. *The People Have Never Stopped Dancing: Native American Modern Dance Histories*. Minneapolis: University of Minnesota Press.

"The Story behind the Graham Google Doodle." Available online: https://www. google.com/doodles/martha-grahams-117th-birthday (accessed July 19, 2021).

Thomas Wood, Marnie. 2009. *Graham Technique*. Personal essay. July 3.

ABOUT THE AUTHOR

Blakeley White-McGuire is a New York-based dancer, choreographer, writer, and educator. Critically acclaimed as a principal dancer with the Martha Graham Dance Company (2001–16, 2017), she has embodied the most iconic roles of twentieth-century modern dance including *Appalachian Spring*, *Chronicle*, *Deep Song*, *Errand into the Maze*, *Frontier*, *Lamentation*, and *Rite of Spring*. As a leading practitioner of the Graham technique, she has contributed her embodied research to three historical reimaginings by distinguished Graham alumni: *Ardent Song* with Professor Susan Mclain, *Imperial Gesture* with Associate Professor Kim Jones, and *Notes on a Voyage* with Professor Peter Sparling. Ms. White-McGuire has performed on international stages including Carnegie Hall, the Metropolitan Opera House, Beijing Opera House, Theatre du Chatelet, Paris, Sadler's Wells, London, the Hollywood Bowl, Vatican City, and the Herodion in Athens, Greece. During her tenure with the Martha Graham Dance Company, she

FIGURE 19 *Blakeley White-McGuire and Abdiel Jacobsen in* Errand into the Maze. *Photograph by Christopher Jones.*

was consistently listed among *Dance Magazine*'s "Best Performances." Ms. White-McGuire was honored to be the featured dancer in Google's "doodle" honoring Martha Graham and to have received the prestigious Premio Positano Leonide Massine Prize for Contemporary Dance Performance as well as the Italian Career Achievement Award.

Ms. White-McGuire has created original dances which have been presented by The Museum of Arts and Design, Downtown Dance Festival, Jacob's Pillow's INSIDE/ OUT, Baton Rouge Ballet Theater, the American Dance Festival, Dancing Human Rights, Oxford, UK, Movement Migration, and with the visual art/dance collaborative "The Tongue of The Flame." Blakeley leads masterclasses and creative residencies worldwide. Her writings expressing the twenty-first-century dancer experience have been published by The Dance Enthusiast, Dance Films Association, *Dance Magazine*, and *Performance Research Journal*.

Ms. White-McGuire holds an MFA in Interdisciplinary Arts from Goddard College, Vermont. She has served on the faculties of New York's famed High School for the Performing Arts, The New School, The Martha Graham Center, and Purchase College. She is currently Adjunct Professor of Contemporary Dance at Hunter College in New York City, and serves on the faculties of The Ailey School, Paul Taylor's American Modern Dance, and Lincoln Center. She leads professional development and consults on circular design for the New York City Department of Education and is an official regisseur re-staging Martha Graham's repertory internationally for the Martha Graham Center.

ACKNOWLEDGMENTS

Dana Mills

Anna Brewer

Oliver Tobin

The Martha Graham Center of Contemporary Dance and community

Hunter College

The Ailey School

Sandra Kaufmann and the Loyola University Chicago

INDEX OF NAMES

INDEX OF SUBJECTS